DIVIDEND INVESTING

A Beginner Guide to Learn Dividend Investing, Build Your Passive Income and Financial Freedom

BY
LUCAS BUNN

© **Copyright 2019 by Lucas Bunn**
All rights reserved.

This document is geared towards providing exact and reliable information with regards to the topic and issue covered. The publication is sold with the idea that the publisher is not required to render accounting, officially permitted, or otherwise, qualified services. If advice is necessary, legal or professional, a practiced individual in the profession should be ordered.

- From a Declaration of Principles which was accepted and approved equally by a Committee of the American Bar Association and a Committee of Publishers and Associations.

In no way is it legal to reproduce, duplicate, or transmit any part of this document in either electronic means or in printed format. Recording of this publication is strictly prohibited and any storage of this document is not allowed unless with written permission from the publisher. All rights reserved.

The information provided herein is stated to be truthful and consistent, in that any liability, in terms of inattention or otherwise, by any usage or abuse of any policies, processes, or directions contained within is the solitary and utter responsibility of the recipient reader. Under no circumstances will any legal responsibility or blame be held against the publisher for any reparation, damages, or monetary loss due to the information herein, either directly or indirectly.

Respective authors own all copyrights not held by the publisher.

The information herein is offered for informational purposes solely, and is universal as so. The presentation of the information is without contract or any type of guarantee assurance.

The trademarks that are used are without any consent, and the publication of the trademark is without permission or backing by the trademark owner. All trademarks and brands within this book are for clarifying purposes only and are the owned by the owners themselves, not affiliated with this document

TABLE OF CONTENTS

Introduction: 1
    Why Do Companies Pay Dividends? 10
    The Dividend Advantage 12
    The All-Important Dividend Dates 17

What Dictates Dividend Policy? 22
    Business And Dividend Life Cycles 23
    Stock Versus Cash Dividends... 27

Dividends Yields And Ratios.. 35

Buying Your First Income Stock 42
    Industries To Hunt For Dividend Stocks 55

Doing Your Homework 62
    Printed Materials 64

Building Portfolio 74
    How To Structure A Low-Beta Dividend Portfolio ... 74
    How To Build A High Dividend Growth Portfolio 78
    Exchange-Traded Funds For Dividend Investors 83

Generating Income From Stocks... 97

The Importance Of Diversification 106
    Choosing High-Yield Stocks... 114
    Developing Your Stock Portfolio 118
    When To Sell A Dividend Stock....................................... 125

How To Manage Your Portfolio To Control Risk 137

Strategies For Safe Portfolio Withdrawals......................... 146
    Portfolio Withdrawals In A Low-Yield Environment
    153
    Portfolio Withdrawals In A Low-Yield And High
    Valuation Environment.. 156

DISCLAIMER

It would be ideal if you recognize that various sorts of ventures include fluctuating degrees of risk. In this manner, there can be no affirmation that the future execution of a speculation, investment, technique, style, framework, or item made reference to straightforwardly or in a roundabout way in this book will be gainful or equivalent chronicled or foreseen execution level(s), or be proper for your own circumstance. In addition, you ought not expect that any dialog or data contained in this book fills in as the receipt of, or as a substitute for, customized venture guidance from its writers or some other speculation proficient. To the degree that a peruser has any inquiries in regards to the appropriateness/reasonableness of a particular issue and additionally venture talked about in this book for his/her individual circumstance, he/she is urged to counsel with the expert advisor(s) of his/her picking. Although dependent on conditions drawn from an assortment of case accounts, all characters and occasions depicted in the models utilized in this book are anecdotal and are not proposed to depict a specific individual or occasion.

INTRODUCTION:

WHAT IS DIVIDEND INVESTING?

Newton's third law of movement has a pragmatic capacity to assist us with understanding material science as well as the impacts and outcomes that market cycles have on speculator conduct. The possibility that you will "buy and hold" through any market decay, secure in the information that business sectors consistently recoup as your portfolio worth evaporates before your eyes, is unadulterated jabber! This is confirmed by the wild, however defective "buy high, sell low" speculator conduct that Wall Street flourishes with. In any case, imagine a scenario where financial specialists held stocks that gave come back from two sources: price gratefulness and dividends. Stock prices change; they generally have, and they generally will. While you will be unable to depend on the arrival from stock price thankfulness, you can rely upon the arrival you will get from dividend payments. Dividends show up each quarter, basically as a general rule. Furthermore, you don't need to sell the stock to get the dividend. When gotten, the unmistakable dividend can be reinvested, used to broaden your venture position and hazard, or used to help your way of life.

A dividend is an appropriation of the benefit earned from company operations or venture action that is paid to investors. A company's top managerial staff pronounces money dividends intermittently (quarterly, semiannually, or every year), and dividends can be paid to investors as money or as extra portions of stock. While money dividends are exceptionally normal, stock dividends are less normal and are typically pronounced when the executives of a company need to reinvest the money created from company operations to develop the company. At the point when financial specialists buy partakes in a company, they get stock endorsements demonstrating the quantity of offers they have obtained. On the off chance that that company pays a dividend, each offer they claim qualifies them for a proportionate portion of the all out dividend comparative with the absolute number of offers remarkable.

Many built-up open organizations pay money dividends and have a dividend approach that is notable to their financial specialists. A portion of these organizations have been paying money dividends for a very lengthy timespan. Banking was one of the primary ventures to create in the

Introduction: What Is Dividend Investing?

United States. The Bank of New York began paying dividends over two centuries back in 1785. Citicorp, probably the biggest bank on the planet, began paying dividends in 1813. The prominent S&P 500 Index is comprised of 500 of the biggest U.S. organizations over each significant industry bunch in America. This list data is counted and distributed consistently by Standard and Poor's Quantitative Services. While there are actually a great number of U.S. organizations whose stocks are exchanged on significant trades, just a couple of stocks from every industry are incorporated into the S&P 500.

As a major aspect of a balanced speculation plan, stocks can be a shrewd method to develop your reserve funds. You may utilize the cash earned from stocks to pay for school, to buy your first home, or even to kick off your retirement investment funds. Individuals who start putting something aside for retirement while they are youthful can store up a significant fortune. The more youthful you start, the more youthful you might be the point at which you resign. Numerous individuals attempt to buy stock when the price per offer is low. Obviously, they trust that the price per offer will go up after some time, expanding the estimation of their venture. A few speculators sell their stocks when the price per offer goes up. Other individuals clutch stocks in any event when the price rises. Nobody knows without a doubt how much the price of any stock will rise or fall later on. This vulnerability is the explanation that stocks are dangerous speculations. The more you find out about a specific company, however, the better thought you'll have about its opportunity of succeeding. Provided that you are going to sell, you need to sell high. Selling isn't the best way to profit from stock, be that as it may.

You can likewise utilize stocks as an approach to gather a customary paycheck. Numerous organizations pay dividends to stockholders. The more cash you contribute, and the better the company does, the higher these payments will be. Most dividends are paid quarterly (like clockwork). However, a few organizations pay them month to month or every year. In the event that your objective is acquiring dividends, your methodology won't be centered around buying low and selling high. Absolutely you need to get as a lot of money flow as you can from your dividends. Rather than profiting at the same time, however, you need to make a relentless pay from your stocks. Thus, you won't do very as a lot of betting. There is nothing of the sort as a hazard-free stock, yet a few stocks are far less unsafe than others.

Introduction: What Is Dividend Investing?

Organizations that have demonstrated track records in their fields are most alluring to dividend speculators. Preferably, these ought to be organizations that have offered stock to general society for a significant stretch of time too. Get your work done, so you know how well the stock has performed over its history. Stocks that have bit by bit expanded in an incentive after some time show that a company is steady, however developing. This doesn't imply that the price per offer has never gone down. About all stocks experience probably some high points and low points, yet the most secure organizations show growth after some time. Stocks that expansion in esteem rapidly are known as growth stocks.

Normally these organizations are extending and are relied upon to see quickly expanding benefits or pay. These are the ventures that individuals need to buy low and sell high. They may pay low dividends, or may not pay dividends by any stretch of the imagination since the board would want to reinvest benefits over into the company. While this course of action may appear to be a terrible arrangement for the stockholders, the objective is to make the company more grounded. This could imply that the company is spending that cash to grow new innovations, include areas, or contract more staff to serve their clients. On the off chance that these progressions help the company to procure considerably more cash over the long haul, its stock is probably going to ascend in esteem. Not every person loves buying a stock that doesn't pay dividends, however. If you need to win dividends, ensure that the stock you buy is from a company that offers these standard payments.

Huge, set up organizations with stable benefits are bound to pay dividends than those that are as yet developing. Dividend ventures may not appear as energizing as growth stocks. Owning growth stocks can be somewhat similar to being on an exciting ride. One day the price may go far up; the following it may tumble to underneath its beginning price. It may even go here and there commonly. You won't see as a lot of progress in the everyday estimation of stocks that pay dividends. This doesn't imply that their worth won't ascend after some time, however. Now and again, you may even observe a fast increment in the price per portion of a dividend stock. Similarly, for what it's worth up to a company's administration to decide if to pay dividends, the measure of the dividend that will be paid is likewise dictated by the executives. Expanding benefits could prompt expanded dividends. However, a powerless economy could make a company cut them. Most organizations attempt to increment or if nothing else keep up their dividends to live up to their stockholders'

Introduction: What Is Dividend Investing?

desires. A drop in the dividend sum could make stockholders sell, and the stock worth could fall.

Getting paid is the reason we put resources into organizations, and we can get paid in two different ways. We can procure a capital gain on a venture if the price rises – you buy it at $25, and if all goes well, the stock hits $50 a few years after the fact – fantastic – that is called an undiscovered gain. In the event that you, along these lines, sell the stock, it turns into an acknowledged gain. The other way we get paid is more unsurprising and reliable than the stock price – this is payment as a dividend. Dividends are regularly paid on a quarterly premise and are controlled by the governing body of the organizations you claim.

As a financial specialist, when you claim a dividend-paying stock, you are for sure a proprietor and are qualified for a bit of the net benefits the company acquires. What's more, shareholders are compensated for their interest in a company by getting dividends, which is a sure dollar sum chosen by the directorate each quarter. Each company's dividend is extraordinary, and the sum paid is regularly a sign of how the company is getting along monetarily and the strategies of the directorate, to the extent returning benefits to shareholders. A few organizations don't pay dividends – they keep their income to extend business or contribute cash as they see fit as opposed to returning it to you. Regularly progressively develop organizations, in the wake of leaving a long growth stage, will start a dividend and afterward attempt to develop it every year to fulfill shareholders. Microsoft is a genuine case of what was previously a tech startup that developed its business for two or three decades before starting a dividend and compensating shareholders with income. It currently pays one of the highest and quickest developing dividends in the innovation area.

Again, as financial specialists, we can get paid by a capital gain as well as by getting a dividend – the mix of the two decides our total return. In the event that you possess a stock that began the year at $25, and it rose to $28, you earned $3 in capital appreciation (undiscovered capital gain). On the off chance that it likewise paid you $1 per share that year in dividends, your total return was $4, or 16%. That likens to 12% in capital appreciation and 4% in dividend payments. It's critical to take note of that all through stock market history, dividends have spoken to 40% of the total return of the stock market. Along these lines, if you claim stocks that don't pay dividends, you are previous a possibly exceptionally huge segment of your anticipated return.

Introduction: What Is Dividend Investing?

Clearly, when we buy a stock, we have no clue how it will perform. We don't have any assurance we will, in the long run, win a capital gain. A company's dividend is ordinarily substantially more unsurprising. A company that pays a dividend will, for the most part, do so paying little respect to how the stock price performs at whatever year or the condition of the economy. Of course, if business turns extremely harsh, as it accomplished for some organizations in the ongoing Great Recession, the company may need to suspend, decrease, or even wipe out a dividend. In any case, most organizations attempt to reliably pay a dividend, however, to likewise develop the dividend a seemingly endless amount of time after year.

The consistency and trustworthiness of the dividend is the thing that ought to draw in you to a company. Indeed, there are numerous different characteristics to search for in a company, and they will be talked about in later sections, however the company's capacity to pay its dividend and its history of ideally raising its dividend every year can reveal to you practically all you have to think about how it is getting along monetarily and furthermore give you a sign that the governing body is sure about the company's future as well – raising the dividend is an indication of a steady and developing business.

There are numerous organizations that have paid steady and developing dividends for a considerable length of time. Some have even paid dividends reliably for a long time or more. These organizations are frequently alluded to as Dividend Aristocrats or Dividend Achievers. Organizations like Procter and Gamble, Exxon Mobil, and Johnson and Johnson, to give some examples, have had a great history of paying and raising dividends. It is soothing for shareholders to realize that in spite of the high points and low points of the stock market, these blue-chip organizations have paid dividends paying little respect to market conditions. Shareholders can reinvest the dividends once again into the stock, contribute somewhere else, or, in the same way as other of my resigned customers, pull back a portion of their dividends to help spread everyday costs.

Why do companies pay dividends?

The vast majority of the stock market is comprised of thousands of organizations that are very little – under $1 billion in market capitalization. These organizations regularly don't pay dividends as they want to clutch their money and reinvest it in their own organizations to extend or put resources into innovative work. Then again, settled enormous top organizations that have been around for a

Introduction: What Is Dividend Investing?

considerable length of time and have a background marked by progress normally remunerate shareholders with dividends.

The enormous effective organizations in the stock market universe, for the most part, need to choose how to manage their profits each quarter (the board of directors chooses) and they think about the accompanying as feasible choices:

- Pay off debt. A company can utilize profits to pay off debt to diminish intrigue payments.

- Repurchase shares. A company can buy back its shares in the event that it feels they are a decent worth. At the point when a company repurchases its very own shares, it diminishes the quantity of shares held by the open, which means that regardless of whether profits continue as before, income per share will rise.

- Reinvest. A company can put profits once again into its business as a means to develop or store innovative work.

- Issue and increment dividends. A company can share profits with its shareholders by paying them money dividends. The company's strategy will be dictated by the board of directors. If the board of directors is expert growth, it will, for the most part, vote to hold profits, repurchase shares or pay off debt. In the event that it is increasingly disposed to share its riches, it will give dividends so all proprietors can share in the accomplishment of the company.

The Dividend Advantage

The pros of owning dividend-paying stocks:

- Own moderate, stable organizations. Organizations that pay reliable dividends are normally run in a genuine traditionalist way with an accentuation on conveying steady, unsurprising profit and dividends to shareholders. These organizations have generally been in presence for a considerable length of time, developed and developed profit enough to at last pay dividends, and the board at that point looks to moderately oversee growth to proceed to pay and build the dividend.

- Income. This is the preferred fundamental position of owning a dividend stock – you get salary,

Introduction: What Is Dividend Investing?

commonly quarterly, and you can decide to reinvest it in your portfolio or use it to help your way of life. It is an incredible favorable position, especially for retirees.

- Income growth. Solid organizations that pay dividends and have a reputation of expanding profits likewise as a rule increment dividend payments in any event enough to keep pace with expansion – think about this as a compensation raise every year, or an expansion in the lease you charge an occupant provided that you are a proprietor. In contrast to a bond, which doesn't expand its payout over the life of the bond, dividends are frequently expanded by 6% or all the more every year. This is awesome for all investors and especially for more youthful retirees who might be worried about living quite a few years in retirement and need to outpace expansion.

- Lower risk. Since dividends are ordinarily paid by progressively settled organizations, one could state there is less risk than owning a stock that doesn't pay a dividend. Also, since capital gains are flighty, at any rate catching a dividend each quarter gives dividend investors some reward for holding a stock, and it can improve execution, especially during a sideways or declining market. The pay fills in as a pad in a bear market and a kicker (additional benefit) in a buyer market.

- Lower unpredictability. Most dividend stocks, especially since they draw in preservationist buy-and-hold investors, show less instability than the market itself. If one takes a gander at the beta estimation of a stock (unpredictability perusing), numerous strong dividend payers show a low beta perusing, which should speak to all investors. To be sure, a portfolio that loses not exactly the market itself in terrible years, because of low beta, and pays dividends, can be attractive.

- Two potential outcomes for gains. As a dividend shareholder, you can benefit from getting the dividend, and you can likewise benefit if your stock ascents to show a price gain. Not at all like the proprietor of a non-dividend paying company, you can profit by both the dividend and potential capital gain – which can make for an attractive total return as time goes on.

Introduction: What Is Dividend Investing?

- Share in the company's prosperity. In the event that a company doesn't pay a dividend, as a shareholder, you are compelled to sell stock each time you have to pull back cash or to really be remunerated for the growth of the company. Selling can include charge outcomes (capital gains). A dividend shareholder takes part in the achievement of the company each quarter by getting a dividend payment without selling shares.

- Grow the number of shares you possess consequently. Since dividends are generally paid quarterly, on the off chance that you needn't bother with dividend payments to enhance your way of life, you can naturally reinvest your dividends in the company or use them to buy other strong dividend payers. The upside of not utilizing other money (outside your portfolio) to expand your share possession is engaging.

- Inflation support. Dividend-paying stocks have generally been one of the main solid ventures that really keep pace with expansion (land is another). Not at all like bonds and other fixed payment ventures, dividends, as a rule, rise every year, at any rate as much as expansion, which can be a tremendous favorable position over a lifetime of contributions.

- Attractive salary in a low-yield condition. Since financing costs stay at truly low levels because of accommodative national banks, dividend yields comparative with different speculations stay exceptionally attractive. One can, in any case, discover strong dividend payers with current yields over 3%. Moreover, a large number of these organizations have been raising their dividends by 6% or all the more every year. With CDs, currency markets, and securities paying by nothing, dividends give genuinely necessary developing income.

- Lower charges comparative with bonds or land salary. Qualified dividends are as of now exhausted at a most extreme pace of 15%, and the rate drops to zero for some lower salary workers who are in the 10% to 15% common personal assessment section. This can be an attractive preferred position when contrasted with premium earned on corporate securities or land rental salary – saddled at the higher conventional annual duty rate.

The All-Important Dividend Dates

For the most part, quarterly, each company's board of directors figures out what size and kind of dividend ought to be dispersed, assuming any. If you don't mind, note that no open company is required to pay a dividend, paying little heed to its past dividend history, or regardless of whether it has just declared its next payout sum and payment date. Most organizations in great budgetary standing are committed to keeping up (and regularly expanding) their dividend payouts, be that as it may, so they are hesitant to decrease or quit paying dividends except if completely vital. Dividends are typically paid on a customary timetable, and you should know about some basic dates.

If you effectively possess an arrangement of dividend stocks, making note of some basic dates for each company you claim can dispense with certain false impressions (why the stock dropped on the day it went ex-dividend, for instance), and it can likewise enable you to ascertain precisely when payday shows up and the amount you will get from each company you possess. What's more, you may likewise get a reward as well as an expanded dividend. We should investigate probably the most significant dates in the life of a dividend-paying stock.

Affirmation date: This is the date the company's board of directors declares it will pay its next quarterly dividend. This is normally made open on the company's Web website, and the revelation additionally incorporates the payment date and the date of record.

Trade date: When you buy a stock, this is your trade date, and the total dollar sum you paid for the stock (cost premise) is additionally critical to know for assessment purposes. In any case, you don't take responsibility for shares on the date of procurement – you possess the shares after the trade settles, three business days after the fact.

Settlement date: The date of settlement date is when the buy and deal exchange is finished between the buyer and the seller. Settlement for most stocks is on the third business day, which is three business days after the trade date. The seller has three days to convey the shares to you, and you have three days to give the money to cover the exchange.

Record date: This is the date that you should be on the company's books to be perceived as a proprietor of record to get the upcoming dividend payment. Your buy needs to "settle" before the record date so as to get the dividend. In the event that you buy the company before the record date, however, the trade settles a short time later, you won't be viewed as a shareholder of record, and the seller who sold you the shares would get that one final dividend payment, not you. Again, you should be recorded on the company's books so as to get the dividend, and that means ensuring you buy the stock before the ex-dividend date, so you are a shareholder of record.

Ex-dividend date: A stock goes "ex-dividend" the day it trades without the upcoming dividend. This means in the event that you buy shares before the ex-dividend date, you will get the upcoming dividend, and on the off chance that you buy shares after it goes ex-dividend, you won't get the dividend (the seller will). The explanation is, again, that in the event that you buy the stock after the ex-dividend date, you won't be perceived as a shareholder of record by the company when the time has come to pay the dividend.

The basic date to recall is the ex-dividend date, and it is two days before the record date. This includes the three-day settlement period made by the stock trade, and it's critical to comprehend what occurs during this period, especially when a stock trades ex-dividend. At the point when a stock goes ex-dividend, the buyer of the shares on that date won't get the upcoming dividend, yet the individual in question will buy the stock at a price less than the dividend that will be paid. Since a dividend is worth returned to a shareholder, on the off chance that you won't get it, you should pay less for the stock than the individual who buys it with the upcoming dividend "included." For example, if a company pays a dividend of $1 per share, on the day the stock opens for trade, ex-dividend, it will trade somewhere around $1 to perceive the upcoming dividend is excluded in the buy. Without a doubt, different variables will impact the development of the stock on that day, yet notwithstanding, it will trade lower by $1, comparative with where it would have regularly traded if the dividend had been incorporated.

Payment date: This is the date that the shareholders of record will get the dividend. For most financier or ledgers, the payment will, as a rule, hit your record and be naturally cleared to the currency market. In the event that you decide to reinvest your dividends naturally, at that point, you will buy new shares of the stock right now as opposed to accepting a money payment. The payday for generally U.S. organizations shows up four times each year, for

Introduction: What Is Dividend Investing?

the most part once per quarter. Some outside stocks will pay dividends just more than once every year.

A few investors trust it is to their greatest advantage to buy a stock with the dividend, before it going ex-dividend, or sell a stock after the ex-dividend date, so as to catch the dividend. However, this has neither rhyme nor reason. In the event that you buy the stock only preceding the company going ex-dividend, you are paying the "extra" dividend sum, which is incorporated with the price in any case. In like manner, if you sell the stock after it goes ex-dividend, so as to get the dividend, you will sell it at the balanced, lower price (by the careful measure of the dividend), to mirror the way that you will get the dividend – not the buyer. Along these lines, don't let accepting the upcoming dividend payment or not impact your choice when to buy or sell, since it is truly disputable. There are no "free snacks."

WHAT DICTATES DIVIDEND POLICY?

Management decides if it will disperse earnings as a dividend or reinvest all earnings to advance the business plan of the company. The proportion of dividends paid out to investors versus the measure of earnings held is known as the payout proportion. Changes in charge law and financial specialist inclination can impact choices in the corporate boardroom in regards to how a lot of benefits to hold or to pay out to investors as dividends. In any case, dividend expands regularly linger behind an expansion in earnings since management will need to be sure that another higher dividend payment will be economical going ahead.

Thinking back over market history, we can see that dividend approach and payouts have remained generally relentless and that any change in dividend yield has had much more to do with the fluctuation at stock prices than with changes to dividend strategy made by corporate directors.

Management is typically extremely hesitant to lessen dividends in light of the fact that a cut is frequently seen as an indication of monetary

What Dictates Dividend Policy?

shortcomings. In any event, during the Great Depression, companies were reluctant to cut dividends. From 1929 to 1932, dividend yields took off on the grounds that most companies kept up their dividends as stock prices fallen in the accident. Be that as it may, as stock prices rose from 1933 to 1936, dividend yields fell—despite the fact that companies were really expanding the dividends they paid. This opposite connection between dividend yield and price was especially apparent during the immense positively trending market run from 1982 to 1999. Companies expanded dividends consistently over the period, really expanding dividends paid by just about 400 percent. However, the dividend yield fallen to notable lows since stock prices expanded by 1,500 percent.

Every so often, a few companies do run into issues and cut or overlook their dividend payments. However, this is the special case as opposed to the standard. The normal dividend-paying company keeps up the dividend payout it sets up as well as pursues an approach of relentlessly expanding its dividend as earnings increment.

BUSINESS AND DIVIDEND LIFE CYCLES

Business life cycles are most impacted by access

to assets and capital. A company's prosperity and development are likewise influenced by a large group of outside factors—rivalry from companies in a similar industry, financial conditions, and in any event, changing shopper inclinations.

There are 6 phases in a company's development that impact its dividend strategy:

1. In the start-up phase, somebody puts cash for stock in the business to create items, enlist workers, pay for gear, and lease space. It isn't bizarre for a company to collect seed cash from proficient investors and enter the start-up phase with a hundred or more representatives. A little company needs to furrow all profits once again into developing and culminating its business model to endure.

2. In the event that the company dispatch is fruitful, it will enter the early growth phase. As the interest for its items or administrations expands, sales and profits increment. The company will still need to reinvest all cash flow and benefit to accomplish aggressive scale.

3. In the late-arrange growth phase, the company continues to develop and may start to pay a little dividend, generally 10–15 percent of earnings. This is an unmistakable sign to

What Dictates Dividend Policy?

investors that the company has arrived at a degree of solidness in profits and cash flow important to help a dividend.

4. In the event that the company is all around run, it will enter the development phase. Its pace of growth may slow as contenders take a portion of the company's market share. Companies at this stage, by and large, increment their dividend payout proportion to roughly 30–40 percent of earnings.

5. Companies can continue to extend even as they arrive at their development phase, yet their growth rate, as a rule, eases back quantifiably. Well-run develop companies can continue to be aggressive powers in their particular businesses for quite a long time or even a few ages. It is during this phase, companies will, in general, increment their dividend payout proportions to 50–60 percent of earnings, which furnishes investors with liberal dividend pay.

6. In the last stages, numerous companies neglect to improve—to keep their upper hand. These companies will enter the decay phase, and except if they rehash themselves, they will, in the end, stop to exist. In this phase, as sales and profits decay, they will, in the long run, decrease or dispose of their dividend payouts.

NOT ALL DIVIDENDS ARE CREATED EQUAL

The rights and advantages of a stockholder rely upon the sort of stock the individual in question possesses. The two primary classifications of stock are common and preferred.

Common stock is the most prominent and generally held form of stock. Most by far of the stocks recorded in the United States are common. Investors who hold common stock have the keep going case on the earnings and resources of a company. Common stockholders are qualified for a share in the profits of the company as dividend payments and appreciation through an expansion in the stock price, which reflects growth in the estimation of the company's benefits. After starting issue, common stock has no fixed dollar esteem; the stock price rises and falls with the company's fortunes. Common stockholders can profit more from a company's thriving or lose more from a company's affliction.

Though the dividend payout on common stocks is variable, preferred stocks pay a fixed dividend, and proprietors are qualified to get dividends before any dividends are disseminated to different shareholders. Preferred stock proprietorship may likewise qualifies shareholders for preferred resources of the company in case of disintegration. Most firms have just one issue of common stock. However, they may have a few issues of preferred stock.

Stocks with the first inclination in the dispersion of dividends or resources are called first preferred or preferred A; the following in the arrangement is called second preferred or preferred B, etc. The fixed dividend on the preferred stock is paid-out from profits (current or gathered), and a company may not pronounce or pay a dividend on the off chance that it doesn't have profits. In the event that the dividend is discarded, at that point, it is said to be "falling behind financially." Most preferred issues are viewed as combined in light of the fact that dividends that are not paid amass to be paid later. There are noncumulative preferred issues whose dividends don't need to be made up whenever missed. Furthermore, a few issues have a transformation highlight that enables the preferred stock to be changed over to common.

STOCK VERSUS CASH DIVIDENDS

A few firms pay stock dividends notwithstanding or in respect of cash dividends. Stock dividends are a dimension of recapitalization and don't influence the advantages and liabilities of the firm. There is a

Dividend Investing

misguided judgment that stock dividends increment the capacity of the firm to develop. Numerous investors accept that stock dividends save cash and really enable the firm to reinvest more for growth. Due to this conviction, numerous stocks trade higher in the wake of paying a stock dividend. Be that as it may, stock dividends don't build the gaining intensity of the company.

In the event that a financial specialist gets extra shares from a stock dividend (and the speculator doesn't have the choice to take the dividend in cash), there is no duty outcome until the financial specialist sells the stock. For instance:

Model: Assume you buy 100 shares of XYZ Company at $10 per share for a total speculation of $1,000, and the company chooses to pay a stock dividend of 10 percent a year later. After the stock dividend, you would possess 110 shares. For duty purposes, your new "adjusted cost basis" on the shares you currently possess is determined by taking your unique venture of $1,000 and isolating by the new number of shares, or 110, to land at an adjusted cost basis for each share of $9.09. If you choose to sell a couple of months after the fact for $12 per share, you will utilize this adjusted cost basis to figure your assessable gain. In this model, you would have a gain for each share of $2.91 and a total gain of $320.

Such an excess of being stated, the idea of paying dividends is currently being exhibited as another advantage.

THE KINDNESS OF STRANGERS

Accepting your stock has ascended in price since the day you got it; how would you profit by this expansion in your riches? You could get against your shares, however then you're truly utilizing another person's money, and the stock is simply guaranteed. Regardless you need to repay the credit, in addition to intrigue, some way or another. On the off chance that you ever need to spend the money, you need to sell the stock. So as to sell your shares, you need to discover somebody to buy them. By far, most of stock exchanges are basically trades by investors selling similar stocks to and fro among themselves. Prices change as their suppositions change about what each share is worth to them. They ascend as a buyer attempts to allure a proprietor to sell, and they fall as sellers attempt to draw in a buyer.

Dividend income, then again, doesn't rely upon the graciousness of outsiders similarly that appreciation does. Dividends are driven principally by the capacity and ability of a company to share its profits with its shareholder proprietors. They are attached all the more near the business itself and are less dependent upon the enthusiastic reaction of investors to world or market occasions. What is a baseball card worth? That relies upon the profession of the ballplayer on the card and the card's irregularity, however—most significant—it relies upon what a gatherer is eager to pay for it. What's the estimation of a work of art? Vincent van Gogh made due on presents, yet his Irises sold at sell-off in 1987 for $53.9 million. Regardless of whether it's a baseball card, a well-known painting, or a growth stock, the main way a financial specialist can profit by its appreciation is to discover somebody who will buy it.

Investors holding stocks for the income they give, then again, enjoy a continuous favorable position that "unadulterated growth" investors don't—they get the opportunity to keep their shares! Clearly, when you've sold your shares, it's another person's stock. You never again have a stake in the fortunes of the company. Any advantages and profits that pursue—just as the future appreciation in share price—are of no further an incentive to you. Obviously, you don't really need to sell all your stock on the double and can hence continue to enjoy a portion of the

What Dictates Dividend Policy?

favorable luck that may continue to visit the company whose shares you're selling. The basic certainty remains, however, that as you sell your shares, you have less of a possession enthusiasm than you did previously. By intermittently exchanging your holdings, you are efficiently decreasing your possession in the very thing that is your store of venture riches. Appreciation has its focal points as well, and, luckily, dividend investors can enjoy the appreciation in the estimation of their shares while they continue to gather the continuous income from their holdings.

At the point when the opportunity, in the long run, arrives to take income from your portfolio to help your way of life, either in retirement or to help settle significant costs, for example, instruction costs, the speculations don't need to be offered to make cash flow. The dividends are as of now flowing cash to you. You essentially need to change its amount you're reinvesting and the amount of it you can bear to spend.

INVESTOR RISK

Investors are reasonably careful about the different risks that can assail a portfolio. Notwithstanding the disintegrating impacts of instability, there's business risk, money risk, market risk, financing cost risk, and expansion

Dividend Investing

risk. Maybe the most slippery risk of all, however, is simply the one that is simply the hardest to shield from—investor risk. Investor risk is the risk that is faced by being human.

It's straightforward the idea that to be effective as an investor, you should buy low and sell high. However, on the off chance that you contribute over a long enough time span to see both rising and falling markets, you'll see exactly how hard it very well may be to carry yourself to really do this. Purchasing at highs and selling at lows is something contrary to progress and can cause your portfolio unsalvageable damage. However, it's phenomenally common. Had you asked those investors who were racing into Internet or other high-flying stocks in mid-2000, after the NASDAQ had recently hopped in excess of 85 percent in 1999, in the event that they thought they were buying high, you likely would have heard a wide range of reasons why this time was unique. There was "another worldview"; the old guidelines of valuation never again applied. Had you solicited numerous from these equivalent investors in mid 2003 in the event that they believed they were selling low following three years of smashing stock market decays, you would probably have known that the market was going to continue falling, the world had changed, and prospects looked grim to the extent the eye could see.

What Dictates Dividend Policy?

Investors were once thought to be "levelheaded," effectively preparing all known market information and settling on choices on the basis of the coherent quest for their own eventual benefits. A whole part of concentrate called conduct fund has jumped up to investigation the topic of how investors truly carry on, and the short answer is that it's once in a while balanced. Nature has "wired" us to respond in specific ways so we can rapidly process information, get designs (like those that happen in nature), and make great, speedy endurance choices. Sadly, a considerable lot of similar ways of reasoning that have demonstrated so accommodating to our endurance as animal types can get us slaughtered as investors.

Passionate reactions, uneven responses to risk and reward, searching for designs where none may exist, accepting our ongoing experience will endure, and pomposity in our underlying decisions are only a portion of the common propensities that can lead us off track. As opposed to attempting to conquer our nature—to defeat the reasoning procedures and propensities that have been woven into our very creatures for centuries—we can attempt to put resources into such a route as to diminish this investor risk and increment our chances of money related endurance. The markets will keep on rising and falling; however, on the off chance that your record doesn't fall so a lot of that, it triggers your base inclination to sell, despite everything you'll be contributed for the bounce back. Indeed, even the most powerful market recuperation doesn't help the investor who has just sold everything before it starts. To procure the long-term performance points of interest of being an investor, you need to figure out how to remain contributed as long as possible. To the degree a lower unpredictability, dividend-based portfolio gives you a venture experience you can live within a wide range of markets, your portfolio is bound to develop into a fortune—and less inclined to confront eradication.

DIVIDENDS YIELDS AND RATIOS

There are a few key yields and ratios that will assist you with surveying a company's wellbeing. How about we survey them so as to eventually construct a superior dividend stock portfolio.

Dividend: The dividend, or dividend rate, is the income that an investor gets from a stock during the year. The cash flow as a dividend is typically paid out of a company's profits. On the off chance that the company doesn't procure enough benefit, it won't be in a situation to pay its dividend. Truly, it can dunk into its cash to pay a dividend during a poor year; in any case, the company needs to acquire enough benefit to continue the dividend. Dividends have truly had a major influence in stock market returns – over 40% of one's total return has originated from dividend payments.

Dividend yield: The dividend yield is determined by taking the total dividends paid in the monetary year and separating it by the share price. For instance, Company XYZ pays a yearly dividend of $2.50. Its stock is cited at $85, so its present yield rises to 2.94% ($2.5/$85).

Dividend Investing

As a company's share price moves higher, the dividend yield drops, and the inverse is genuine as well – essential math. A strong company with a past filled with reliable profits will need to persistently raise its dividend to stay aware of expansion, yet to likewise draw in new investors. Note, a dividend yield clearly doesn't recount the total anecdote about the attractiveness of a stock. A company that has a quite high dividend yield may really be in a tough situation. On the off chance that the stock has dove and the yield bounces accordingly, the market may be telling investors that the company may need to decrease or dispense with its dividend – there is inconvenience. Thus, it's imperative to look past a stock's yield to decide whether it is a commendable speculation.

Dividend growth rate: This is the annualized rate of growth that a stock's dividend will appear for the year. Preferably, the dividend growth rate for a stock ought to, at any rate, stay aware of expansion and ideally outperform it. Many blue-chip companies that have had a past filled with expanding dividends every year show a dividend growth rate of over 6%. Coca-Cola and Procter and Gamble have had a background marked by raising dividends, and they are very adult companies. In any case, in 2015, they are both scheduled to build dividends by 8%. It is essential to take note of that in the present high-

Dividends Yields And Ratios

priced market, dividend growth has been not able stay aware of rising stock prices. Subsequently, the dividend yield on the Dow Jones Industrial Average is a negligible 2.4%, and the dividend profit on the S&P 500 is just 1.8%. Either dividend growth should get considerably in the coming a very long time to make stocks increasingly attractive, or stock prices need to drop (yields ascend) to bring yields nearer to typical recorded levels.

Dividend payout ratio: Dividend payout ratio can be defined as the dividend per share isolated by the earnings per share, communicated as a ratio. Here's a model: In 2014, Coca-Cola proclaimed dividends of $1.22 per share and earned $2.03 per share. $1.22 separated by $2.03 shows a payout ratio of 60%. Along these lines, Coca-Cola is sharing a genuinely heavy segment of its profits with shareholders. Expecting a company is set up and procures reliable profits, it might be the objective of the board of directors to attempt to keep up a certain payout ratio after some time. So as the company develops, so will the dividend and the resulting payout to shareholders. Note, on the off chance that a payout ratio gets excessively high and surpasses earnings, at that point, the dividend will be at risk. Furthermore, a decrease in the dividend is a poor sign to investors about the company's wellbeing. Subsequently, the stock price ordinarily soaks, fully expecting a dividend cut. Then again, a steady dividend payout ratio and a strong dividend strategy will enable a company's share to rise after some time.

Price-to-dividend ratio: The price-to-dividend ratio is the price of a share to dividends paid in the earlier year. This ratio can be utilized to quantify a company's potential as a venture or as a valuation instrument for the general market. The accompanying diagram shows that in the early piece of the only remaining century, investors were eager to pay around $23, overall, for every dollar of dividends, and as of now, they are paying practically twofold that price – the 2015 price-to-dividend ratio is roughly $45. The high current perusing, much the same as the raised CAPE ratio, has regularly been seen at past market tops. In 1999, at the tallness of the tech bubble, the price-to-dividend ratio hit a pinnacle of over $68. While we have not approach that level, we are near the level come to in 2007, preceding stocks dove half.

Earnings per share: This is a company's benefit isolated by the quantity of extraordinary shares. This measure is viewed as one of the most significant determinants of a share's price and worth. Here are the means by which it is determined utilizing a basic model: If a company

Dividends Yields And Ratios

earned $4 million of every one year and had 2 million shares extraordinary, its EPS would be $2 per share.

Price-to-earnings ratio: The price-to-earnings ratio is the present price partitioned by earnings per share. Commonly, a lower price-to-earnings ratio equivalents better worth.

CAPE ratio: The CAPE ratio depends on a price-to-earnings model promoted by Yale financial expert Robert Shiller. This consistently adjusted price-to-earnings ratio is a valuation measure generally applied to the S&P 500 record. It is characterized as price isolated by the normal of ten years of earnings (moving normal), adjusted for swelling. It is essentially used to survey likely future returns from stocks and can give an accurate sign with respect to whether stocks are priced high or low comparative with chronicled valuations. The present perusing in mid-2015 is 27. This grandiose level plainly shows prices are high comparative with consistently adjusted earnings.

Debt-to-equity ratio: The debt-to-equity ratio rises to a company's present moment in addition to long-term debt separated by shareholder equity. A high debt-to-equity ratio, for the most part, shows a company has been forceful in financing its growth with debt. This can bring about unpredictable earnings because of the extra premium cost. On the off chance that a great deal of debt is given to fund expanded operations (high debt-to-equity), the company might generate more earnings than it would have without the financing. If this somehow happened to expand earnings by a more noteworthy sum than the cost of the debt (premium), at that point, shareholders will profit. Notwithstanding, the cost of debt financing may exceed the return the company generates on the debt through speculation and business exercises and could turn into a weight. Ordinarily, the lower the debt-to-equity ratio, the less helpless a company will be during recessionary occasions. Specifically, pay consideration regarding long-term debt commitments as a company might be required to make intrigue payments to debt holders for a long time.

Cash flow per share: Cash flow per share is a proportion of a company's monetary quality and is determined as pursues:

Cash Flow per Share = (Operating Cash Flow – Preferred Dividends) separated by Common Shares Outstanding

Numerous budgetary experts place more accentuation on the cash flow per share an

Dividends Yields And Ratios

incentive than on earnings per share. The highly regarded money related firm, Value Line, for instance, utilizes cash-flow projections for a company to help decide the future stock price extend over the coming 3 to 5 years. While earnings per share worth can be effectively controlled to show up more positive than it truly is, consequently placing its dependability being referred to, cash is progressively hard to adjust, bringing about what a few investigators accept is an increasingly accurate proportion of the quality and supportability of a company's business model.

Again, since the cash flow per share mulls over a company's capacity to generate cash, it is viewed by certain investigators as a progressively accurate marker of a company's money related circumstance than the earnings per share metric. Cash flow per share speaks to the net cash a firm delivers, on a for each share basis.

BUYING YOUR FIRST INCOME STOCK

You may have heard this saying, "it takes money to profit." This announcement is particularly obvious with regard putting resources into stocks. Before you can start acquiring dividends, you should pick a company wherein to contribute your cash. Effective companies make the best ventures, yet di¬fferent individuals measure a company's accomplishment in di¬fferent ways. For example, a few investors may believe that an effective company is the pioneer in a specific industry. Others may pass judgment on progress by to what extent a company has been in business. Still, more may the accomplishment by a company's worth or market capitalization—which is determined by duplicating the share price by the total number of shares. A company that remaining parts solid even in a feeble economy is regularly observed as wise speculation. You might need to search for a few of these characteristics in the company you pick.

Your quest for dividend stocks should start with an attention on companies that have a past filled with conveying reliable, rising dividends. This should help relieve risk by picking companies that are probably not going to diminish or take out dividend payments. You can additionally place the chances in support of you by seeing total return potential (dividends in addition to capital gain), and not just concentrate on current yield. Numerous investors commit the error of just picking stocks dependent on current dividend yield, yet they neglect to think about other significant factors on a company's monetary record. Most remarkably, they ignore the dividend payout ratio, potential growth of the dividend, and earnings consistency.

Here is a summary of a portion of the characteristics you should search for in a dividend stock as you assemble your portfolio. At least 20 stocks in different enterprises would be perfect, with an accentuation on companies that convey unsurprising earnings and dividend growth in any monetary condition. Search for a few, if not all, of the accompanying attributes:

• Dividend profit ratio of 65% or less and a reliable payout ratio in the course of recent years. The proportion of the number of a company's profits are paid out in dividends is a key consideration in picking a dividend stock for your portfolio. You are searching for not just a payout ratio of 65% or less; however, a ratio that has remained genuinely steady over numerous years. The lower the number, the better, however, you do need a company that pays out a considerable lot of its earnings – a number that is too low ought to be a notice that the objectives of the board of directors probably won't line up with your income needs.

Clearly, if the payout ratio gets excessively high and profits can't cover the dividend, the company and its dividend might be in a tough situation. Along these lines, leave some edge for blunder – search for a to some degree moderate payout ratio so that if business falters for a quarter or two during a downturn, the dividend will at present be kept up and ideally expanded. You can discover the payout ratio for a company utilizing Value Line, or other online Web locales like www.dividendinvestor.com. Or then again, you can compute the payout ratio yourself. Take the stock's yearly dividend and separation it by the agreement earnings per share.

• Dividend yield half more prominent than the S&P 500's returns. The current profit for the S&P 500 is 1.8%, so search for a stock with a current yield of at any rate 2.7%. This is exceptionally clear – you need income past what the market is paying. Another benchmark to take a gander at is the 10-year Treasury yield – you need income past what the 10-year note is paying. With this key loan fee sitting at abnormally low levels, around 2%, it's genuinely

Buying Your First Income Stock

simple to discover quality stocks yielding more than securities.

• 10 consecutive long stretches of dividend growth, averaging 5% or all the more yearly. At the very least, a company's normal yearly dividend growth ought to be more prominent than the current rate of expansion (2% or more). Numerous very settled companies like AT&T, Verizon, and Consolidated Edison, to give some examples, pay a lot higher than normal dividend yields; however, don't grow their dividends by much every year. This can be adequate; however, preferably, you need dividend growth to, in any event, keep pace with expansion. Furthermore, you need to assemble a portfolio of companies offering both dividend growth or more normal current yield. Companies that have grown dividends by and large 5% or all the more every year for as far back as 10 years should give you the certainty that they can support and grow their earnings and dividends in any event, during troublesome financial occasions (the company has demonstrated it is very much overseen). It is critical to perceive how a company's dividend performs during a full monetary cycle – extension and downturn.

• 10 consecutive long periods of earnings growth averaging 5% or all the more every year.

Dividend Investing

This is legitimately connected to your quest for steady dividend growth since companies that can't grow earnings reliably won't have the option to grow dividends either. You will obviously observe some cover in these two classes.

• Predictable earnings that can withstand recessionary times. In the event that you approach Value Line either with your very own membership or maybe through your neighborhood library, the earnings consistency rating appointed to each stock is useful. This is a number starting from 0 then to (100 being the highest rating) and the strong names that give practical, predictable earnings through all sorts of challenges, get a high positioning. It shouldn't come as an unexpected that names like Coca-Cola, PepsiCo, Procter and Gamble, Johnson and Johnson and Colgate-Palmolive, all procure close to ideal scores for earnings consistency.

• Price-to-earnings ratio at or underneath the market's various. Most budgetary Web destinations like www.finance.yahoo.com will show you either a year trailing PE ratio for a stock or a year forward PE dependent on earnings gauges. You can contrast this ratio with the market's different (Dow Jones Industrials or S&P 500). It is prudent to search for companies that have a PE ratio at or beneath the numerous of the market. Notwithstanding, remember that extraordinary companies may trade at a premium numerous over the market, and they regularly merit the premium.

• An easy to-comprehend business model selling items or administrations well-known to you. I like to claim companies that my customers know about – companies like Kimberly-Clark, Procter and Gamble, Coca-Cola, and Johnson and Johnson all have items that you will discover in your own home and these stocks can fabricate a strong establishment for a portfolio. Expecting they meet different criteria you are searching for, it's decent to possess companies in a business that you get it.

• Cash on the balance sheet. I like to buy companies that have steady earnings growth, pay growing dividends, and have a lot of cash on the balance sheet. The cash can be utilized to administration or pay down debt, reinvest in operations, repurchase shares, or even help briefly pay the dividend. Many blue-chip dividend payers have a cash crowd in the billions of dollars, which gives solace to investors. For instance, in mid-2015, Procter and Gamble have $10 billion in cash, Chevron – $14 billion, PepsiCo – $7 billion, Intel – $15 billion, and Johnson and Johnson has over $33 billion in cash on its balance sheet.

- Low beta. Beta is an estimation of a stock's unpredictability comparative with the entire market. The S&P 500 own a beta of 1.0, so a stock with a beta perusing under 1.0 will show less instability than the market. A low-beta portfolio can help limit the unpredictability in a portfolio and smooth out what can regularly be an uneven ride. The beta for a specific company can be found on about any money-related Web website. Fortunately, numerous dividend stocks in the shopper staples, utilities, or medicinal enterprises appear underneath normal beta statistics: Colgate-Palmolive – 0.43, Coca-Cola – 0.47 General Mills – 0.6, Johnson and Johnson – 0.48, and AT&T – 0.56, to give some examples.

Anything that is critical to you see some key numbers and choose what your criteria will be for contributing. You will need to search for a decent yield; however, don't pick a monetarily risky company since it offers a high yield. On the off chance that a yield appears to be a lot higher than others in the business, make certain to check the budget summaries cautiously. You can likewise check a stock's budgetary soundness rating with a free guide like Morningstar.

The dividend yield is one of the most significant numbers that you'll be thinking about, and it's likewise essential to note whether a company has routinely expanded its dividends after some

Buying Your First Income Stock

time. Company X offering a 3 percent yield today could be a superior interest over the long haul than Company Y offering a 4 percent yield—if X is reliably expanding dividends. For instance, suppose that you put resources into ten shares of each company at $100 each. In your first year, X will pay you back $3 per share or $30, versus Y's $4 per share or $40. Nevertheless, imagine a scenario in which in five years, X's dividend has expanded to $7 per share. However, Y's is still $4 per share. Presently you are making $70 every year or a 7 percent return on your interest in X, yet getting 4 percent from Y. What's more, stock prices regularly increment when dividends increment, so your interest in X could be worth significantly progressively after some time.

Records are accessible to stocks that have ceaselessly expanded dividends after some time. Stocks on the S&P 500 Dividend Aristocrats have expanded their dividends consistently for the last twenty-five years; Mergent's Dividend Achievers stocks have expanded their dividends reliably for at any rate ten years. In case you're hoping to gather a customary paycheck from your stocks, you may likewise need to consider the dates that a stock's dividends have been paid before. A few investors like to balance their ventures, so they are getting checks, in any event, a few times per month.

Dividend Investing

Notwithstanding a company's dividend yield, another figure to search for is the return on equity (ROE). Equity is the sum left from the company's total resources (like cash, hardware, or land) after you subtract the liabilities or debt. Return on equity is basically a proportion of how a lot of expert t a company makes every year for each dollar that is contributed. A 15 percent ROE shows that a company earned $15 off professional for each $100 that stockholders have contributed. You can compute the return on equity all alone on the off chance that you have two numbers: the measure of the company's net income and shareholders' equity. "Net" just means the sum that is left over after the sum total of what reasonings have been made. To discover the ROE, isolate the net income by the shareholders' equity. You can discover this information on a company's income articulation and balance sheet. Think about the ROE for as far back as quite a long while, and contrast it with others in a similar industry. A few investors search for this number to be at a specific least, for instance, 10 percent or more.

Earnings per share (EPS) is a comparable proportion of profitability. Yet, this number estimates how much benefit a company made for each share of stock. Consider a company's payout ratio too—what amount of their ace t would they say they are paying out in dividends? While it's incredible to get however much genius t as could reasonably be expected from a company that you put resources into, recollect that if a company pays out a lot of its cash, it probably won't have enough left to endure startling difficult times. Numerous specialists suggest stocks with a payout ratio of under 60 to 80 percent. Picking your first stock can be a touch of overpowering. To make the procedure less distressing, take as much time as necessary. Tight your decisions down to a couple of different companies; at that point, think about their minimum speculation amounts, dividend yields, share prices, earnings per share, and return on equity.

When you are prepared to make your stock purchase, you should choose whether you need to utilize a representative or purchase your stock directly from the company. Managing a merchant has changed significantly in the course of the most recent few decades. Online business firms have made buying stock simpler. Numerous online firms charge very low expenses for stock purchases. Having an online money market fund likewise makes dealing with your speculations a more straightforward issue. In any case, you might need to think about buying direct. Merchants make money by charging investors commissions on stock purchases. Not paying a commission means a greater amount of your money goes directly into the speculation.

Several companies offer direct stock purchase plans (DSPPs), here and there called direct venture programs (DIPs). If you are keen on a specific company, you can visit its site to see whether it offers a DSPP. Because you are buying direct, however, doesn't mean you won't need to pay any charges whatsoever. A few companies charge an arrangement expense, a purchase charge each time increasingly stock is purchased, and charges for selling stock. These charges are often not exactly those of numerous financier firms, be that as it may.

Each company has its own minimum speculation amount for stock purchases. A few companies require a minimum stock purchase of $50; others have minimums of $500 or more. Numerous companies will forgo this charge in the event that you are happy to focus on a month to month purchase plan until you arrive at the minimum amount. A company with a minimum purchase amount of $500, for instance, will, for the most part, enable new investors to purchase stock in the event that they consent to pay $50 every month for ten months. At the point when the ten months have passed, you would then be able to choose if you need to continue contributing the $50 every month or stop.

The money for DSPPs is normally pulled back directly from the investor's ledger. The conclusion will be made around the same time each month. You simply need to ensure that the money to pay for the stock is in the record before that time. A few companies will enable you to pay with a money order, however many charges an extra expense in the event that you utilize this sort of payment.

You can likewise purchase stock through one of the numerous different online associations. First Share, Money Paper, and ShareBuilder are only a couple of these assets that help new investors begin. These mediators aren't stockbrokers; however, they will charge a specific amount for their administrations. You won't pay them directly, yet rather pay somewhat higher expenses when buying stock through their sites. Much of the time, you will improve by buying your stock directly from the company you pick, however, make certain to contrast every one of the expenses in question and every choice. When you have purchased stock in a company, you can start acquiring dividends. You will, at that point, need to choose what you need to do with your dividends. In the event that your underlying venture is a little one, your dividends won't indicate much first and foremost. This doesn't imply that your dividends don't have esteem. Whatever the size of your speculation, you may choose that the most ideal approach to grow your venture is by utilizing your dividends to buy increasingly stock.

Most companies that offer dividends make it simple for their stockholders to buy progressively stock with their dividends. A dividend reinvestment program (DRP or DRIP) enables you to fold your dividends into extra stock purchases. Your dividends at that point start exacerbating or creating earnings from past dividends. When you pursue a DRP, you won't need to accomplish a thing to make these buys. They will happen naturally at whatever point dividends are paid. Your month to month or quarterly dividend payment may just be sufficient to purchase a small amount of a share, yet after some time, these fractional shares can include. The longer you reinvest your dividends, the more stock you will gather.

In the event that you need to start a DRP, yet the company doesn't offer a direct stock purchase plan, you can work around this test. Essentially purchase your first share (or anyway numerous shares you should buy to meet the minimum purchase amount) through an agent. When you claim in any event one share, you would then be able to request that the representative issue you a stock authentication (the dealer may charge an expense for this administration). You would then be able to give a duplicate of this archive to the company's shareholder administration division to set up your DRP.

Most DRPs offer investors the chance to make discretionary cash payments (OCPs) with low minimum amounts. Maybe your preferred auntie sends you $25 consistently on your birthday. If this is true, you can utilize this money to make an OCP. Discretionary cash payments are another approach to increment both your number of shares and the amount of your dividends. Numerous representatives will presently set up a DRP for their customers. Remember that there is a trick to going to this course. If you need to buy extra stock through an OCP, you should pay a commission on that purchase. At whatever point conceivable, it is smarter to utilize the money that would go to a commission towards your stock purchase.

Industries to Hunt for Dividend Stocks

The most attractive industries of the market to find strong dividend payers are commonly those that generate high cash flow and earnings per share and pass this on to shareholders as

Dividend Investing

dividends. One could contend that an investor could essentially pick top dividend payers from a bunch of industries and have sufficient expansion with a lot of income and growth potential. While there are twelve sectors that include the S&P 500, my feeling is that you could claim dividend stocks from half of these sectors and still have a lot of broadening and higher yearly dividend payments as well.

It is sensible to start your pursuit in attractive cash-flow industries where companies have a past filled with compensating shareholders. Industries like nourishment and drinks, oil and gas, telecom, tobacco, and utility champion for dividend plays. Again, because of www.dripinvesting.org, you can channel through names and industries that meet your criteria for nothing and fabricate an attractive portfolio.

Consumer Staples

The sector of consumer staples is made up of companies delivering as well as selling fundamental items, for example, nourishment, refreshments, tobacco, and family things. Consumer staples are products that individuals can't or reluctant to dispense with from their spending limits, paying little mind to their cash-related circumstances. These stocks are considered non-repeating, which means they are always popular, regardless of how inadequately the economy is performing. We tend to purchase consumer staples at a generally consistent level, paying little mind to price. Consumer staples can be a decent alternative for investors looking for gradual growth. Companies that exceed expectations in this industry incorporate Procter and Gamble, Kimberly-Clark, General Mills, Johnson and Johnson, and Coca-Cola.

The consumer staples sector is the most loved of investors looking for security when market instability increments. In particular, the nourishment and drink sector has truly been a specific zone of intrigue in view of the inelastic nature of its hidden items.

Tobacco

Tobacco stocks have demonstrated to be among the strongest, downturn confirmation values for a long time. Volume decays for the enormous tobacco companies are the same old thing, and this has been a common pattern for quite a while. However, luckily for tobacco shareholders, the rest of the clients are happy to bear heavier cost trouble than they have previously. At the point when these companies report their earnings, the outcomes may not be pivotal; however, they will likely continue to keep the stock prices moving higher and the dividend growth as well.

Oil and Gas

Oil and gas is a class of stocks that produce or supply vitality. This sector incorporates companies associated with the exploration and development of oil or gas saves, oil and gas boring, or integrated power firms. Performance in the sector is, to a great extent, driven by the market interest for overall vitality. Vitality makers will do very well during times of high oil and gas prices, yet will acquire less when the estimation of vitality drops. Moreover, this sector is delicate to political occasions, which generally have driven changes in the price of oil.

The vitality business isn't any not quite the same as most product-based industries as it faces long times of blast and bust. Boring and other help firms are highly reliant on the price and interest for oil. These firms are a portion of the first to feel the impacts of expanded or diminished spending. In the event that oil prices rise, it sets aside effort for oil companies to evaluate land, set up rigs, take out the oil, transport it, and refine it before the oil company sees any benefit. Then again, oil administrations and penetrating companies are the first on the scene when companies choose to start investigating.

Oil and gas prices change regularly, and there are numerous elements that decide the price of oil. Be that as it may, it extremely all comes down to organic market. Request ordinarily doesn't change excessively. However, it will during downturns, which makes this sector and the stocks it contains, more unstable than most.

Telecom

Consider telecommunications a machine hung together by complex networks, phones, cell phones, and Internet-connected PCs – this worldwide framework contacts almost we all. It enables us to talk and work with about anybody, paying little heed to where they are on the planet. Telecom companies make this conceivable. In the not so distant past, the telecommunications business has involved a club of huge national and local administrators. In any case, over recent decades, the industry has been cleared up in fast deregulation and advancement. In numerous nations around the globe, government syndications are currently privatized, and they face new contenders. Conventional markets have been flipped around as the growth in versatile administrations outpaces fixed lines, and the Internet starts to supplant voice as the staple business. It is difficult to keep away from the end that size issues in telecom.

It is a costly business; contenders should be enormous enough and produce adequate cash flow to assimilate the costs of extending networks and administrations that become out of date apparently medium-term. Transmission frameworks should be supplanted as often as possible at regular intervals. Huge companies that claim extensive networks – particularly neighborhood networks that stretch directly into clients' homes and businesses are less dependent on interconnecting with different companies to get calls and information to their last goals. On the other hand, littler players must pay for interconnection all the more often so as to complete the activity. For little administrators wanting to grow enormous one day, the money related difficulties of staying aware of fast mechanical change and deterioration can be amazing. In this way, stay with built-up transporters – Verizon and AT&T ring a bell. An outside holding like Vodafone can likewise offer strong dividends and moderate growth potential in the telecom business.

Utilities

The utility sector includes companies, for

example, electric, gas, and water firms. Since utilities require critical framework, these firms often convey a lot of debt. With a high debt load, utility companies begin to be touchy to changes in interest rates. As interest rates rise or drop, their debt payments will increment or lessening. The utility sector performs best when interest rates are falling or stay low.

While utility stocks are never again synonymous with huge dividends, that doesn't imply that dividends never again matter. Most utility companies still put forth an admirable attempt to guarantee dispersion of cash to shareholders, and comparative with different industries, utilities offer superb income potential. Dividend yields in this sector regularly bid to traditionalist investors and are often observed as rivalry for securities. What you don't have in the utility business, since companies as of now pay out enormous bits of their earnings in dividends, is ideal dividend growth potential. In any case, expecting the current yield is better than expected, and the company builds its dividend every year, utilities are an invite expansion to about each portfolio.

DOING YOUR HOMEWORK

Having the option to recount a list of key information basic to the stock determination isn't a kind of magic incantation for success. You need to really find that information for each stock on your list. Furthermore, in light of the fact that the information is continually transforming, you additionally need to stay up with the latest—ideally quarterly. How much time your research exertion will take relies upon how you do it. Visiting the library and composing or calling for annual reports will unquestionably work. However, you'll invest a great deal of energy gathering information.

In case you're ready to consequently download the information you need directly into a spreadsheet or database, that piece of your research can occur in minutes consistently—while you're resting. It's difficult to envision whatever has accomplished more to facilitate the weight of protection findings for the sole investor than the development of the Internet. The amount and nature of information you can without much of a stretch access from the solace of your own home genuinely boggles the brain. Need an annual report? Snap. Access to government filings? Snap. Prices, graphs, analysis, discourse? Simply click again.

Doing Your Homework

Information that once took tremendous amounts of time and devotion to gather presently hurries to your fingertips down the information superhighway.

Innovation can unquestionably assist you with throwing a more extensive net as you continued looking for winning stocks, yet your definitive accomplishment as an investor will, in all probability, be dictated by how you utilize the information you find, instead of by how you discover it. There are three principal ways in which the information you're searching for will differ.

1. Cost. An astounding amount of information is accessible for nothing, either directly from companies themselves, from government offices like the Securities and Exchange Commission (SEC), or certain Web sites. Financier firms often make some form of research accessible to their clients. Membership administrations differ drastically in price, from the cost of a day by day paper to a great many dollars for each month for far-reaching information and analysis administrations.

2. Format. Information is accessible in print or electronic format. Papers, magazines, and annual reports are recognizable in print. Electronic adaptations of every one of these

distributions are commonly accessible, as are hosts of programming applications and Web sites.

3. Content. Fiscal summaries, balance sheets, and company reports give a rich wellspring of information things, yet you most likely should process the ratios yourself. Some outsider information administrations give precisely this kind of prepared information previously determined for you. Key budgetary ratios, earnings patterns, and per share information are commonly listed, along with analysis and editorial, including rating administrations and lists of explicit security suggestions. The amount of information is normally commensurate with its cost.

The cost, format, and content of a wide range of information sources are quickly advancing, and any endeavor at an extensive listing would be immediately old. By pointing out a couple of options over the range of decisions, we plan to show you an example of the kind of information that is accessible. How you continue will rely upon your degree of interest, assets, inclinations, and ability with PCs.

Printed Materials

Most papers incorporate business areas;

Doing Your Homework

however, their inclusion fluctuates broadly, and their stock and mutual fund listings are often fragmented and list minimal more than the earlier day's price. The Investor's Business Daily and The Wall Street Journal are famous day by day papers for business news.

Barron's

An incredible spot to start gathering information and to stay up with the latest on significant market news is Barron's, a weekly monetary paper. In Barron's Market Week segment, you'll discover powerful stock listings with something other than the ongoing price, including:

- Ticker images (significant for acquiring information and putting inaccurate exchange requests)

- Dividend yield communicated as a level of the current stock price, and the dividend amount in dollars per share

- The price/earnings ratio (P/E), a significant valuation measure

- Per-share earnings information, including a year ago's earnings, the current year's earnings and one year from now's anticipated earnings

Dividend Investing

- Trading volume

- The 52-week low price and high for the security

- A large group of "stock ticker code images" to alarm you to everything from chapter 11 to stock parts

Barron's is much something other than its stock tables. Consistently it's brimming with interviews, feelings, research, and articles on the markets (stock, security, land, item, and outside), the economy, innovation, shared assets, and interesting companies. For the dividend investor, Barron's Market Lab area contains a table listing the week's dividend payments. An ordinary segment, "Discussing Dividends," conveys news and views about what's happening in that edge of the speculation world.

Annual Reports

A company's annual report is a decent hotspot for a considerable lot of the information things you'll require, just as for critique about the company. It ordinarily incorporates a letter from the top executive to shareholders with their view of the significant occasions influencing the company, and their view of the

Doing Your Homework

company's possibilities going ahead. You'll likewise normally find engaging information about the company and its business (or businesses), in addition to a segment that gives all the fiscal summaries, including consolidated income proclamations, balance sheets, cash flow explanations, articulations of shareholders' equity, references, and a report of the free examiners. Perusing the annual report is an extraordinary method to acquaint yourself with a company. Remember, however, that companies attempt to put their best foot forward in their reports to shareholders, so the analysis is probably going to cast the company's situation in the most ideal light. A letter or call to a company's investor relations division is generally the entirety of that is expected to have a free duplicate of the latest annual report sent your direction.

For an apparently less one-sided view of a company's condition and prospects, you can go to one of a few stock rating productions:

- The Value Line Investment Survey gives money related information and key ratios on around 1,700 stocks and rates their attractiveness on a size of 1 to 5 for both wellbeing and timeliness.

- Standard and Poor's Stock Reports offer

discourse and buy/hold/sell suggestions dependent on its STARS rankings for roughly 5,000 traded on an open market companies listed on the New York, American, NASDAQ, and provincial stock exchanges.

- Morningstar made its name positioning common assets; however, it has ventured into stock research through its Stock Analyst Reports on around 1,700 stocks. In the event that you utilize a business firm, it might likewise have an assortment of stock research and proposal information accessible to you. Look at with your delegate to discover what's offered and at what cost.

Internet Sources

Every one of the business newspapers and stock rating administrations simply portrayed is accessible in an online Internet rendition. You can, by and large, likewise get information directly from an interesting company's Web site. Essentially run an inquiry on the company name, go to the company's landing page, and search for the "investor relations" section. Companies' Web sites generally fluctuate as far as their convenience and content; however, most will include:

Doing Your Homework

- The latest annual and quarterly reports (the quarterly report might be alluded to as the "10-Q")

- Recent news discharges and access to a news discharge document

- A schedule of occasions, including arranged shareholder gatherings

- Notes and analysis from late expert gatherings, discourses, or different introductions

A company's Securities and Exchange Commission filings can be found on the SEC's Web site under EDGAR (http://www.sec.gov/edgar.shtml), where you'll find directions for utilizing the EDGAR database. There's likewise the FreeEDGAR Web site (www.freeedgar.com), where you can pursue free preliminaries of different EDGAR Online membership administrations on the off chance that you'd like to investigate the more extensive access to company information they offer. The Reuters Web site (www.reuters.com) provides a company search include with which you can find a ton of nitty-gritty information about an imminent purchase candidate. Under "News and Markets," select "Stocks" and afterward enter the company's image. You'll be offered a

Dividend Investing

selection of views, including Overview, Financials, News, Options, People, Analysts, Charts, and Research. In the Overview, you'll find a current statement, a short portrayal of the company's business, and a couple of things of money related data, including dividends per share, yield rate, price/earnings ratio, and earnings per share. The Financials view shows a significantly more hearty accumulation of data, including income and earnings history, examiner gauges, valuation ratios, dividend growth rates, industry, and sector examinations, and considerably more.

You can likewise enter an image in the Yahoo! Money section (www.finance.yahoo.com) to find a company profile and connections to Quotes, Historical Prices, Charts, Technical Analysis, News and Info, Key Statistics, SEC Filings, Headlines, and Financials, including the Balance Sheet, Income Statement, and Cash Flow Statement. Most financier firms make whatever research is typically accessible to their clients open online as a component of their Web sites, often with news, cites, and other information also. The sources and supply of information accessible on the Internet are quickly growing and evolving. The areas and information depicted here may vary from what you find as you surf the Internet for data, and you may find sites that don't exist as this book is being

Doing Your Homework

written. The purpose of this short stock is basically to illustrate the gigantic amount of information effectively open on the web. While the speed and accommodation of the Internet can be important, be mindful to test the precision of the data you're getting against a certain source before you depend on it all the time to settle on your choices. Awful data can be more regrettable than no data by any stretch of the imagination.

While a few investors enjoy talking about their stock picks in "visit rooms," we prescribe that you adhere to the numbers—not talk room analysis—in settling on your venture choices. Despite the fact that you may gain a few bits of knowledge from sharing thoughts on the web, there have been a lot of accounts of deceitful individuals utilizing their Internet postings to attempt to publicity, impact, or sell stocks. With all the legitimate wellsprings of information accessible, why gamble your well-deserved money on the counsel of an unknown or spontaneous tipster?

SOFTWARE AND DATA SERVICES

There are software programs and data suppliers that convey a practically incredible amount of point by point money related data on for all intents and purposes each traded on an open market stock. They incorporate incredible analysis apparatuses and estimating models, diagramming capacities, and interfaces with spreadsheets and other software programs. They are additionally costly. Designed principally for the requirements of the institutional or expert investor, they can, in any case, be an incredible incentive for these clients regardless of the cost since they make gathering and handling tremendous amounts of data attainable. Except if your portfolio is of institutional size, be that as it may, it's impossible that the run of the mill cost of thousands of dollars for each month would ever bode well for you.

There are software programs accessible for the individual investor; however, many are equipped to assisting with specialized analysis as well as day exchanging. As dividend contributing turns out to be progressively famous, notwithstanding, it would not be astounding to find new items being acquainted that give mechanized access the kinds of ratios and crucial stock information you need. Attractive highlights would incorporate the everyday download of updated information into your computer and apparatuses to separate and rank the stocks in your universe by the criteria you determine.

Doing Your Homework

While Internet access and computer software can let your research generally straightforward and productive, remember the library. Your nearby library most likely has computer offices for Internet access in the event that you'd like to investigate that scene for your research; however, don't have a computer or Internet access at home. Contingent upon their size, numerous open libraries have extensive accumulations of business-related reference materials, often including duplicates of the Value Line Investment Survey, Morningstar Stock Analyst and Mutual Fund reports, and Standard and Poor's Stock Reports. You're probably going to find a duplicate of the current week's Barron's at the library, just as a large group of different newspapers, business magazines, and books. In the event that you find you have the tendency, inclination, interest, and time to do as such, accept the open door to seek after further training in the zone of stock analysis. Numerous individual investors become very talented at perusing and dissecting budget reports, and there are numerous tales about beginner investors uncovering important information that expert investigators have missed. When you find the correct wellsprings of information for you, it's time to utilize your data to characterize the universe of stocks you will follow.

BUILDING PORTFOLIO

How to Structure a Low-beta Dividend Portfolio

Low-beta stock portfolios, shared assets, and ETFs have gained in prevalence lately as investors try to reduce risk in a very unpredictable speculation condition. I think investors are insightful to consider low-beta strategies, and I typically possess low-beta dividend stocks for my oversaw records as well, paying little heed to market valuations. Low-beta stock portfolios by and large requests to moderate and traditionalist investors. For a snappy review of beta, the broad market (S&P 500) has a beta reading of 1.0, and each stock is connected diversely to the market and has its very own beta reading. Beta estimates the volatility of speculation comparative with the market itself. In this way, a portfolio or stock with a beta of 0.75 will be 75% as unstable as the market itself. In this model, if the market were to ascend by 10%, a portfolio with a beta of 0.75 would rise 7.5%. Similarly, if the market were to decay by 10%, this lower beta portfolio should just drop by 7.5%. In this way, clearly for traditionalist or moderate investors (typically retirees) who need to reduce volatility, lessening beta bodes well.

Building Portfolio

There have been various investigations looking at low-and high-beta stocks and how they are non-connected during monetary extension periods (buyer markets) and recessionary times as well (bear markets). Most studies have indicated that low-beta stocks typically reduce volatility in a portfolio, yet additionally outperform. The advantage of a low-beta portfolio originates from the low connection with the broad market and the low relationship each stock has to the others in the portfolio. This low connection reduces volatility; however, it doesn't really reduce returns. The main concern, and why you ought to think about a low-beta portfolio – you may have a higher return than the market and lower volatility. This is perfect.

I accept there are a couple of purposes behind low-beta stock outperformance: 1) Low-beta stocks typically pay high and growing dividends, and this additional yield and expanded cash flow every year adds to performance after some time – helping a portfolio to outperform the broad midpoints. 2) Low-beta stocks have gained in notoriety the recent decades as markets have gotten increasingly unpredictable, and investors have become more risk-unwilling. These stocks pull in money, which thusly, helps their prices. 3) Low-beta stocks are typically found in industries where earnings are

Dividend Investing

autonomous of financial volatility. Stocks in the consumer staples or utility sectors (where one will find many low beta readings), for instance, ordinarily have progressively consistent earnings in any event, during recessionary periods as their items or administrations are sought after on a consistent basis. Again, increasingly consistent and unsurprising earnings make low-beta stocks less delicate to market gyrations.

I think it bodes well to concentrate a portfolio in low-beta stocks, especially during times of overvaluation – periods when the CAPE ratio (consistently adjusted price-to-earnings) has a reading great above 16.5 (its recorded normal). The explanation behind this is if valuations are high, or on the off chance that we are in a period where we have had a long, positively trending market run, we realize this pattern will in the long run invert, and an adjustment or bear market will happen. In the event that stocks are expected for a decay, for reasons unknown, however, regardless you need to keep up the introduction to stocks, you could bargain and possess a portfolio of low-beta stocks to ideally reduce the amount of money you will incidentally lose if the general market decreases.

In this way, as opposed to moving totally to cash

Building Portfolio

or (bonds are likewise currently exaggerated), a trade-off is to continue to possess stocks, however, reduce volatility however much as could be expected with low-beta choices. On the off chance that the market thusly decays.

Focal points of a low-beta stock portfolio:

- Less volatility than the market itself.

- Potential outperformance in all sorts of challenges.

- High current and growing dividends. Most low-beta stocks pay decent dividends. This adds cash flow to a portfolio, which additionally assists within general performance in bull and bear markets.

- More unsurprising earnings. Low-beta stocks are typically found in industries with consistent earnings. This consistency draws in investors and assists support with stocking prices.

- A risk-decrease bargain during times of overvaluation. A low-beta portfolio can be an attractive choice to stay invested in stocks, as opposed to selling out totally, when stocks are obviously exaggerated. Since stocks can stay highly-priced, over their verifiable normal CAPE valuation level of 16.5, for a long time, a trade-off is to just move to a portfolio of low-beta holdings. By swapping holdings to low-beta stocks, you can ideally bring down your portfolio's drawdown during a redress or bear market, stay invested, gather dividends, and continue to have price appreciation potential.

To abridge, low-beta portfolios can give risk-loath investors an approach to keep up stock introduction, cash flow, and capital gain potential while generally lessening volatility. Low-beta stocks are especially attractive in exaggerated markets as they ordinarily decrease not exactly the market when patterns turn negative.

How to Build a High Dividend Growth Portfolio

While most dividend investors center around current yield, it is similarly critical to claim companies that show high dividend growth potential. It's conspicuous why investors are pulled in to current yield since this is the yield they will catch promptly, and current dividend yield rates are shown and cited on money-related Web sites and in newspapers. It is rare to find an investor get some information about

Building Portfolio

the future dividend growth of a company – everybody is centered around current yield. Again, this is a mix-up in light of the fact that it is the growth of the dividend that will enable your portfolio to outpace expansion, and a solid dividend growth rate likewise reveals to you the company is progressing admirably and earnings are ample.

At a minimum, I trust it bodes well for all investors to concentrate on both current yield and dividend growth. A blend of the two ought to enable you to have enough current cash flow while ideally additionally furnishing you with dividend growth more noteworthy than swelling – and potentially double the rate of expansion. At present, expansion is going around 2% annually, so a portfolio concentrated on current income, yet in addition to companies growing their dividends by 4% or more is a decent starting point.

We should quickly review a portion of the benefits of putting resources into companies that grow their dividends:

- Compounded dividend growth. The advantages of exponential growth are duplicated by growing dividends. This is on the grounds that both the quantity of shares (from reinvestment) and the dividends per share are growing. The intensity of aggravated dividend growth can provide aggressive returns paying little mind to whether the price of the stock increments.

- Capital protection. Quality dividend-paying companies are more full-grown and stable than most. These stocks typically hold up better in down markets and provide a lot of upside in buyer markets as well.

- Create an income stream. Dividends provide a customary income steam that can be reinvested or help spread everyday costs. Most stocks pay a quarterly dividend, yet a well-developed portfolio of dividend stocks can provide a consistent month to month income stream as well. Dividend growth is particularly basic for early retirees who may need to live off a portfolio in retirement for quite a few years and need to keep pace with expansion.

- Inflation fence. The huge burden of fixed income speculations is that the income stream doesn't grow. Indeed, even a 3% swelling rate will annihilate half of the buying intensity of your head in only 24

Building Portfolio

years. Companies that expansion their dividends provide the capacity to get income that increments and keeps up the obtaining intensity of your head and income.

- Center your quest for Dividend Growth Achievers utilizing the accompanying criteria:

- Dividend payout ratio (EPS %) of 65% or less. The lower the payout ratio, typically, the more space there is to grow the dividend later on, and the more uncertain you are to see a dividend decrease. All things considered, you don't need a payout ratio that is excessively low – you need to put resources into companies that share a sound level of their profits and reward shareholders.

- Dividend yield half more prominent than the market's yield. The S&P 500 is currently yielding 1.8%, so search for companies that are paying at any rate 2.7% in annual dividends and ideally higher.

- Consistent dividend growth. Companies that have accomplished a long history of dividend growth have substantiated themselves during numerous financial cycles (all sorts of challenges). Additionally, don't overlook up-and-comers ("Challengers") who have started to appear in any event 5 years of consecutive dividend increments. Concentrate your pursuit on companies that raise their dividends, all things considered, in any event enough to keep pace with expansion.

- Manageable debt-to-equity ratio. A high debt-to-equity ratio demonstrates a company has been forceful in financing its growth with debt. This can bring about unstable earnings because of the extra interest cost. On the off chance that a great deal of debt is utilized to fund expanded operations (high debt-to-equity), the company might generate more earnings than it would have without outside financing. If this somehow happened to build earnings by a more prominent amount than the debt cost (interest), at that point, the shareholder's advantage as more earnings are being spread among a similar amount of shareholders. Nonetheless, the cost of this debt financing may exceed the return that the company generates on the debt through venture and business exercises and become a lot for the company to deal with. By and large, an entrenched company can drive the risk part of its balance sheet structure to higher rates without stumbling into difficulty. Search for companies that have a low debt-to-equity ratio and look further into the balance sheet (Value Line) to get a thought concerning the amount of the total debt is long-term.

- Low beta. A company's stock price that shows less volatility than the market itself is engaging for preservationist and moderate investors. While volatility is typically not a central factor when picking a stock, a dividend portfolio included low-beta names is attractive, especially when markets are exchanging at a high valuation. I would recommend searching for companies with a beta reading of 0.60 or less. What's more, in the event that you pick stocks with higher beta readings, consider balancing this with some lower beta stocks, so the general volatility of your portfolio is not exactly the market itself.

Exchange-Traded Funds for Dividend Investors

Exchange-Traded Funds (ETFs) needn't bother with quite a bit of a presentation as they have gotten uncontrollably famous in the course of recent years. Somewhere in the range of fifteen years back, truth be told, not many investors had known about them. Presently, most investors know ETFs provide a magnificent option in contrast to conventional mutual funds, and one could likewise contend that a portfolio contained just dividend-paying ETFs is all the stock presentation you have to help arrive at your venture goals. As such, you could contend against owing any individual dividend companies – essentially possess them through ETFs that are involved in the companies you need in your portfolio. I want to have better risk control by owning singular dividend-paying stocks and reduced venture costs as well.

Exchange-Traded Funds (ETFs) started in the late 1980s and immediately gained fame as investors started searching for more affordable and progressively fluid options in contrast to mutual funds. Investors, both institutional and individual, could see the advantages of holding a particular gathering of stocks with lower management expenses and intraday price perceivability. Let us take a look at points of interest and drawbacks of owning dividend-paying ETFs so you can choose in the event that they are proper for you.

Preferences of owning dividend-paying ETFs:

- Diversification. A solitary ETF can offer an introduction to a gathering of values, market portions, or styles. In contrast with a stock, an ETF can follow a broader scope of stocks, or even copy the returns of a nation or a gathering of nations. For instance, you could concentrate on dividend-paying companies in Europe or Emerging Markets or an individual industry. Mutual funds can also be differentiated, yet ETFs can give you quick broadening with the push of a catch on your keyboard.

- Low expenses. ETFs, which are commonly latently overseen, have a lot of lower continuous costs contrasted with other oversaw funds. A mutual fund's cost ratio is typically higher because of costs, for example, a management charge, bookkeeping costs at the fund level, administration and marketing expenses, paying a board of directors, and burden expenses available to be purchased and appropriation. Moreover, ETF charges have even declined further lately as firms like Vanguard and iShares by BlackRock seek latently oversaw dollars where cost

Dividend Investing

is terrifically significant. A few ETFs are accessible for as meager as 0.10% in annual costs. This is short of what one-tenth the continuous cost of numerous effectively overseen mutual funds and can have a significant effect over a lifetime of contributing.

- Trade like stocks. ETFs trade for the duration of the day on an exchange, much the same as any commonplace stock you may buy. Mutual funds, then again, are accessible for purchase or deal toward the finish of each trading day, and you ordinarily need to enter your request about an hour before the end of trading. Things being what they are, you really don't have the foggiest idea what price you will get when you enter a purchase or sell request on a mutual fund – who realizes what may occur on that specific trading day? Since ETFs trade like stocks, they enable you greater adaptability to make purchases and sales during the trading day and not need to hold up until the day's end – and at an obscure price. Furthermore, ETFs trade at a price that is revised for the duration of the day. An open-finished mutual fund is priced uniquely by the day's end, at the net asset esteem.

Building Portfolio

- ETFs can be purchased on edge and undercuts. On the off chance that you are so disposed, you can purchase ETFs, as most stocks, on edge (acquired money) and sell them short as well. This can be a favorable position for examiners, yet in addition for progressively moderate investors who are hoping to support a portfolio to reduce risk. This can be viewed as a preferred position; however, I don't energize theory or using edge for generally investors.

- Dividends are reinvested naturally and right away. Dividends of the companies involved in an open-finished ETF are reinvested right away.

- Capital gains charge presentation is restricted. ETFs can be considerably more assessment effective than mutual funds on the grounds that the greater part of the duty on capital gains is paid simply after the clearance of an ETF happens, and this is at the watchfulness of the investor. Regardless of whether the ETF sells or buys shares while endeavoring to impersonate the bushel of shares it is following, there is typically no assessable circulation to shareholders (not at all like some effectively overseen mutual funds). The explanation behind this is in-kind moves found in ETFs don't bring about a duty charge, and subsequently can be required to be a lot of lower than mutual funds. Mutual funds, then again, are required to appropriate capital gains to shareholders if the administrator sells securities at a benefit. This circulation amount is made by the extent of the holders' venture and assessable as a capital gain. On the off chance that other mutual fund holders sell before the date of record, the rest of the holders split the capital gain, and along these lines, pay assessments regardless of whether the fund declined in esteem and regardless of whether they didn't sell any of their own shares. This can be an extremely horrendous astonishment, and I had had numerous talks with investors who have been stunned when they were appropriated an assessable gain by a mutual fund despite the fact that they didn't sell any shares during the year. It tends to be an intense idea to get a handle on, yet it's unimaginably imperative to remember it happens much of the time. Main concern, numerous effectively overseen mutual funds do not charge proficient, and ETFs, generally, are superbly charge productive – a colossal bit of leeway.

- Lower rebate or premium in price. ETFs trade for the duration of the day at a price near the estimation of the underlying securities, and if the price is fundamentally higher or lower than the net asset esteem, exchange will bring the price back in line. This is not quite the same as shut end funds since ETFs trade dependent on organic market and market creators will catch the price disparity to keep the estimation of the ETF near the underlying securities.

- Predictable income. Dividend-paying ETFs pay income as unsurprising as the underlying shares. Along these lines, if you claim an ETF that is invested in high-quality dividend payers, you can be sure that the quarterly dividends will be passed on to you, the shareholder, as though you held the individual shares. This is significant for retirees or anybody living off the income generated from a portfolio.

Disadvantages of owning dividend-paying ETFs:

- Bid-ask spread can be enormous. As

more specialty ETFs are made, you may really find an interest in a low volume file, and this could bring about a high offer ask spread. You may show signs of improvement price by putting resources into the underlying stocks themselves, not by means of the ETF. In the event that you possess an ETF or are hoping to purchase or sell one that has low volume, make certain to enter a breaking point request as opposed to a market request to be certain you don't get a poor fill because of a huge offer ask spread. In the event that you stick to exceptionally fluid ETFs that have high day by day volume, the offer ask spread won't be an issue. In any case, be cautious with ETFs that put resources into little sectors or outside markets that may have low volume. Search for highly fluid ETFs with billions in assets that trade regularly.

- Costs are higher than owning individual stocks. Most investors contrast trading ETFs and mutual funds, yet in the event that you contrast ETFs with putting resources into a particular stock, at that point, the costs are higher. The genuine commission paid to the agent may be the equivalent, yet there is no worked in management charge for having a

Building Portfolio

portfolio of individual stocks just like we have with ETFs or mutual funds.

- Dividend profits may not be as high as owning individual stocks. Some dividend-paying ETFs have yields that probably won't be as high as owning a gathering of stocks. In the event that you handpick your own portfolio of individual stocks, you can concentrate on the high yielding companies, for instance, and disregard those with lower yields. Be that as it may, when you buy a bushel of stocks by means of an ETF, you are going to follow a broad market or sector typically, and you are compelled to have part proprietorship in each stock in the ETF – even those that may pay dividend yields lower than you need.

- More hard to control risk than with individual shares. If you claim a portfolio of ETFs rather than a portfolio of individual shares, you may find it is increasingly hard to control risk. So as to reduce risk, you don't have the main alternative I often propose, and that is to expel the high-beta stocks from the portfolio as the market becomes exaggerated. These are stocks that have a beta (proportion of volatility) higher

Dividend Investing

than the market itself. Shockingly, with ETFs, you can't sell any of the underlying holdings – you have to claim every one of them. In this way, owning individual shares gives you greater adaptability and risk control.

- More hard to control charges than with individual shares. If you claim a portfolio of individual stocks, you absolutely have a few stocks that have performed superior to anything others, and you may have some that show misfortunes. On the off chance that you have taken an assessable gain in some random duty year and you are hoping to counterbalance the gain with a misfortune, you can sell at least one of your individual stocks to balance the gain. This can be an incredible preferred position when overseeing money for charge proficiency. Be that as it may, with an ETF or mutual fund, you typically just have a solitary cost basis for the whole venture – you can't go into the underlying bin or fund and sell a failure to balance a champ to get a good deal on charges. Most importantly, ETFs offer less assessment adaptability than owning individual shares – and this is essential to think about when overseeing assets in

Building Portfolio

an assessable record.

- ETFs could urge you to trade. Now and again, an investor might be urged to sell a speculation at an awkward time in the event that the person possesses an ETF rather than a mutual fund. Here's a case of how this may occur – assume you claim an ETF and you wakeful to see the stock market and your ETF diving by 5%. You alarm and enter your sell request, and you liquidate your whole holding inside seconds. Diminished, you approach your day just to find that the market really recouped the whole amount later in the day and completed higher. In the event that you had not claimed the ETF, rather, a mutual fund, you would not have had the option to sell during the downturn since you can just sell a mutual fund toward the day's end. You not exclusively would have had a superior price on your deal, however you likewise probably won't have rushed to pull the trigger and sell, on the off chance that you had possessed a mutual fund rather than the ETF. Along these lines, for long-term investors or the individuals who are highly passionate investors (inclined to freeze), as long as the costs are tantamount and the fund is as duty effective as an ETF, you could consider having a mutual fund rather than an ETF. Vanguard has ETFs that mirror a portion of their inactively overseen mutual funds, and a few investors may really be ideally serviced by owning their mutual funds rather than the ETFs.

- Forced to possess companies you don't need. Although I am a supporter of ETFs, it has always troubled me that I have to claim a bit of each company in an ETF, regardless of whether I don't put stock in the company or could never possess the company altogether. Again, when you purchase an ETF you are buying a crate of stocks or securities, and you have to possess ALL of the stocks that are in the ETF – you aren't ready to maintain a strategic distance from a few and pick others as you can with a portfolio of individual shares. In this way, before you purchase an ETF, you should investigate the ETF and see what rate it claims in every individual company, what the top holdings are, and if the ETF possesses companies that you don't trust in or would prefer to keep away from, at that point don't make the purchase. It is hard to find a dividend-paying ETF that will just involve companies that you need,

Building Portfolio

however very simple to find dividend-paying ETFs that have a large portion of their money invested in companies you like. In any case, I should state, it bothers me to try and have one dollar invested in a company I don't have confidence in, and that is always the situation with ETFs – you don't get the chance to pick the underlying companies in the ETF.

- Diversification from ETFs won't moderate risk of misfortune, maybe changeless, during bear markets. While ETFs offer broad broadening like conventional mutual funds, they are not invulnerable to price decays and convey indistinguishable risks from the holdings that involve the ETF. While they have numerous favorable circumstances, conventional ETFs will not the slightest bit control risk during market downturns and are, truth be told, set up to mirror the performance of a list (up or down).

- In rundown, dividend-paying ETFs are utilized by investors to construct a broad-based portfolio or gain introduction to explicit sectors. There are numerous preferences, particularly contrasted with effectively oversaw records and mutual funds. ETFs are a lot

Dividend Investing

of like stocks in the manner they trade, and dominant part is endlessly more attractive than mutual funds for the reasons referred to in this section. Indeed, there are a couple of hindrances, yet the points of interest far exceed any negatives.

GENERATING INCOME FROM STOCKS

There's gold in them there dividend stocks! A perfect income portfolio needs to incorporate a solid portion of these stocks. Securities may have higher yields and generate more cash for every dollar invested; however, their income streams are fixed and don't keep pace with swelling. Since dividend-paying stocks do keep pace with swelling, we have found that a balanced methodology of contributing about portion of an income portfolio in securities and the other half in high-yielding dividend-paying stocks works best.

On the off chance that dividend-paying stocks ought to be a piece of the perfect income portfolio, at that point, for what reason aren't progressively resigned investors utilizing them? There are essentially two reasons:

1. Most stocks have low dividend yields.

2. Stocks are unstable and are viewed as too risky

There are numerous books and online assets where you can find information about how to put resources into bonds. Stocks that pay

Dividend Investing

dividends tend to build dividends after some time. Furthermore, the prices of stocks, for the most part, increase in value over long timeframes, allowing the income investor to reposition a bit of the stock portfolio to expand income. Dividend stocks are likewise commonly less unpredictable than run of the mill growth stocks. During the multi-year Y2K bear market, dividend stocks really held their worth superior to their growth partners. Since dividend-paying stocks from enormous companies in mature industries don't fall as much in a market decrease, they are viewed as protective stocks. They tend to hold their worth since investors buy these kinds of companies as they rescue of increasingly risky growth plays. The resulting deluge of cash into these issues causes them keep up their worth even in declining markets.

Income investors should concentrate their hunt on dividend stocks that have yielded high enough to generate the income they require. In the event that you need an income stream equivalent to 4 percent of invested capital, at that point, you should search for stocks with yields in the 4 percent run. There are a large number of stocks, so to make your activity of finding the correct dividend stocks simpler, we recommend you rationally bunch them into three particular yield classifications.

Class 1. The Low Yielding Stocks

These are the stocks that have **a dividend** yield of not exactly the yield on the S&P 500 Index. Sometimes, the yield on the S&P 500 Index is about 1.52 percent. Despite the fact that they do pay a dividend, they tend to reinvest the greater part of their earnings to cultivate growth in esteem through price appreciation. These stocks are extremely suitable for growth investors; however, they may neglect to meet your income requirement.

Classification 2. The Medium Yielding Stocks

These are the cases with dividend yields that are proportional to the list's yield or higher and tend to be companies concentrating on giving a balanced return from the two dividends and price appreciation. When screening for stocks, stocks with yields that are in any event, 150 percent of the record's yield is targeted. They are focused on their dividend program and payout from 30 to 50 percent of earnings in dividends. You can shop in this gathering for income, yet recall that the object of your pursuit is to find stocks that reach your income requirement, so you should concentrate on stocks with higher yields.

Classification 3. The High Yielding Stocks

Dividend Investing

These are the cases with yields today in the 4 to 5 percent extend or higher and are companies that are, for the most part, in mature industries that emphasis on giving investors returns through dividends. They payout 50 percent or a greater amount of their earnings to draw in investors with a high dividend yield. Mature industries that fit this class are utilities, banks, pharmaceuticals, vitality, and land venture trusts (REITs). As referenced before, the dividends from REIT stocks and vitality (MLPs) don't fit the bill for the new lower tax rate. Try not to neglect to incorporate them for consideration, however, in light of the fact that their high yields are convincing, and their after-tax yield may more than balance the difference in the tax on these cases versus dividend stocks which do meet all requirements for the new lower tax.

You can find stocks with yields more than 4 percent from mature companies in specific industries like utilities that emphasis on drawing in investors with their high dividend yields. You can likewise find underestimated stocks with delicious yields that have dropped out of support with investors. As a rule, their prices have declined while their dividends have stayed steady, expanding the stocks' yields simultaneously. Break down these circumstances cautiously to decide why the

Generating Income From Stocks

stock has declined in price and if its dividend is secure. There is often a fundamental business motivation behind why the stock price is declining: neglecting to meet earnings desires, declining income, expanding debt levels, and so on. Your main responsibility is to decide whether the price decrease is a brief misfortune or part of a bigger negative pattern. In case you're sure that the valuing modification depends on brief conditions that you see improving, at that point, you may have found a chunk of gold!

Since you get the chance to spend just the income you hold after you pay your taxes, it is basic to break down your speculation choices cautiously to attempt to downplay your tax trouble. In spite of the fact that we accept each resident should pay their fair share of taxes, paying too much is a direct loss of riches. Reserve funds vehicles and government and corporate security interest will be taxed at your highest common income tax rate, and the interest you gain will be included with all your other income to decide your tax bracket. Then again, qualifying dividends will be taxed at a lower inclination rate of 5 or 15 percent, contingent upon your income level and tax bracket.

Conventional investments like bonds, munis,

endorsements of stores, and money market records are great income generators, yet they don't build their income after some time to assist you with keeping pace with rising costs due to swelling. Stocks provide swelling assurance through a growing stream of dividend payments (dividend stocks) and growth in esteem through price appreciation; however, they bomb the well-being of chief test due to their wide swings in price.

The perfect income portfolio for a great many people shares these essential attributes:

- The investments in the portfolio are sheltered.

- The income generated by the portfolio is unsurprising.

- The income is adequate to help your way of life needs.

- The income ascends after some time to keep pace with rising costs due to swelling.

A great many people who are taking income from their portfolios are at a phase in their lives when they are never again willing or ready to construct their fortunes once more. Often, this income stream is the contrast between (An) an agreeable way of life and the genuine feelings of serenity they longed for as they anticipated their "brilliant years" and (B) subsistence living described by simply attempting to make do with a fixed benefits and Social Security. The more we depend on the income from our portfolios, the more unsurprising it must be. Bills have a method for appearing each month, regardless of whether we have income coming in or not. Regardless of what's new with interest rates, stock prices, or the economy, the income check needs to appear in the letterbox every month on the grounds that the bills must be paid. So the profit from your investments must be safe, and your income portfolio head should be kept up, so your income continues to flow continuously. In the event that you can't depend on the income to land as required, you can't plan and can't generally rely on keeping up a specific way of life.

Resigned investors comprehend that as long as their chief is protected, it will continue to generate income to help their ways of life. Keeping up their capital is directly identified with keeping up their profit. As much as they need income, they're not set up to interpretation of much risk to get it. Think about your venture capital as the motor that generates income. In the event that you expect an income rate of 5 percent, at that point, $1,000,000 of capital could bring forth $50,000 in annual income. In the event that you lost $200,000 of your capital base, at that point, your littler motor would generate just $40,000 in annual income. As you lose capital, your capacity to generate income is disabled. What number of people do you realize who resigned on a fixed income and afterward battled to stay aware of the consistently rising cost of living as the years passed by? On the off chance that you live long enough, what once appeared as though a royal whole could undoubtedly transform into a beggar's wage as expansion makes prices walk constantly higher. Today you would need to spend nearly $5.71 to buy similar products and ventures that could be purchased for $1.00 in 1970. This is what might be compared to having a record that was worth $100,000 in 1970 psychologist in incentive to $17,508!

Relatively few individuals are in a place that grants them to lose more than 80 percent of their genuine buying force and still keep up their way of life. A dollar may at present be a dollar years from now, yet you just need to think back over your very own lifetime to perceive how the buying intensity of every dollar can blur away. What amount did you pay for your first new vehicle or first house? What amount would a comparative vehicle or house cost you today? Swelling influences the price of all that we use in our everyday lives. An endless mug of espresso cost a quarter 25 years back; today, some espresso at Starbucks costs $1.95, and there is nothing of the sort as a free top off. Keep in mind; our optimal income portfolio should be protected, not simply extend the figment of well-being. To do that, the turn-over it produces must ascent to keep pace with swelling.

THE IMPORTANCE OF DIVERSIFICATION

Probably the most ideal ways to keep your overall investment risk as low as conceivable is expanding. This means spreading your money between various different sorts of investments. On the event that you put the entirety of your reserve funds in stocks, you could lose most or even the entirety of your money if the stock market crashes or if the company you've invested in leaves business. Despite the fact that there is normally a recuperation after a stock market crash, it can set aside some effort to occur. Consequently, keeping a specific level of your money in safe investments, for example, testaments of the store or government securities, is keen. By doing this, you ensure that you will always have a specific amount of reserve funds that can't be lost. How would you know when it is a decent time to put resources into the stock market? You will never know without a doubt what will occur in the stock market tomorrow. A decent method to tell how the stock market is getting along today is considering stock indexes. These lists of stocks incorporate the Dow Jones, the Nasdaq, and the S&P 500. On the off chance that you watch the news, you have most likely heard reporters talk

The Importance Of Diversification

about the Dow Jones Industrial Average. This number is a weighted normal estimation of thirty of the greatest stocks accessible today. At the point when a reporter says that the Dow has ascended by twenty-five, the person in question means that the cost of buying these stocks today is $25 more costly than the cost of buying them yesterday. In like manner, lost twenty-five points means that the stocks are $25 more affordable than they were at the end of business the earlier day. Numerous investors will hold on to purchase stocks when these indexes are low, wanting to buy a strong stock at a limited price.

You can't depend on the Dow or some other list to disclose to you how a particular stock is getting along. You can notwithstanding, utilize these indexes to get a thought of how the general market is performing. On the event that you are considering buying stock in a particular company, watch its encouraging along with the companies on the Dow over some undefined time frame. On the off chance that the Dow is progressing admirably while your company is rising in esteem, it could be an indication that the company is a savvy pick. On the off chance that your company continues rising in any event when the Dow falls a piece, it could be a far and away superior sign that it is a wise speculation decision. In the event that your company is falling as the Dow stocks are rising, in any case,

Dividend Investing

make certain to find out why and utilize that information when you think about your purchase. In the event that your stock is doing gravely when different stocks are progressing nicely, what will befall your venture if the market crashes?

Destroying stock market misfortunes have happened a few times since forever. The crash of 1929 denoted the start of the Great Depression. Throughout the following, not many years, stock qualities went down in excess of 80 percent from where they had been in the late 1920s. More than a quarter-century after the stock market crash of 1987, individuals still talk about October 19 of that year. Presently known as Black Monday, this was the day when the Dow Jones Industrial Average sank 508 points. It lost 22.6 percent—the greatest misfortune at any point found in a solitary day of trading. The year 2008 additionally demonstrated to be a terrible time for the two stocks and the economy by and large. On October 15, 2008, the Dow dropped 7.8 percent. These misfortunes were inevitably recuperated, be that as it may, as the stock market has continued to increment in esteem over the long term.

Provided that you need to put resources into the stock market, you can't wipe out the risk. You can lower it, in any case—again, by utilizing

The Importance Of Diversification

enhancement. The gathering of investments wherein you contribute your money is called your portfolio. Your portfolio may incorporate stocks, securities, and testaments of store (CDs). Your stock portfolio comprises of the considerable number of shares of stock you hold in different companies. In the event that you put all your money in a solitary company, you could lose any or every last bit of it if that stock does ineffectively. Be that as it may, if you separate your money down the middle and buy stock in two different companies, you will be fit as a fiddle in the event that one of them suffers a misfortune.

Monetary specialists differ about how much an investor ought to broaden when dividends are the objective. If you are attempting to make customary income from dividends, the companies you pick will share numerous characteristics practically speaking. You need to pick companies with demonstrated track records and promising fates. While broadening is significant, you would prefer not to expand so a lot of that you take a risk on a company that is battling.

At the point when a company's stock goes down, a few people buy as much as they can. The objective of these investors is making a huge profit if the company skips back. They consider

Dividend Investing

a to resemble this just like a potential bargain. As an income investor, you won't look for this kind of stock; however, rather, you will be centered around dividends. At the point when a company starts battling, dividends are often the main thing to go, as the company needs to utilize this money to help pay its costs.

In any case, you can and should try buying different stocks. The gathering of stocks from which you pick might be littler, yet broadening is significant. It can't be said enough: there is no assurance that any stock will progress admirably. You could put resources into one hundred unique companies, and every one of the one hundred could fail. It is far-fetched yet conceivable. Simultaneously, consider what happens when you spread your money among only ten stocks. In the event that one company's stock goes down in esteem, regardless, you have nine different stocks that could keep up their share price. Some of them may even go up in worth and o¬ set your misfortune. Similarly, a few companies' dividends may diminish while other companies' payments may increment. Numerous monetary specialists exhort against contributing in excess of 10 percent of your money in stock from a single company.

In spite of the fact that dividends are your primary objective, you ought to likewise watch

The Importance Of Diversification

out for the price per share. On the off chance that the share price diminishes, so does the amount of your speculation. You needn't bother with the price per share to increment too rapidly; however, you don't need it to fall an excess of either. This worry drives us to an undeniable inquiry: Should you sell your stock if the company starts doing inadequately? The appropriate feedback relies upon a few elements. To begin with, consider the explanation that share price dropped. Is the share price an impression of a momentary issue that can be survived, some portion of a general market change, or is it a sign of more concerning issues in the company? Is there new information that shows the company isn't as steady as you suspected when you originally purchased? Provided that this is not false, you might need to sell. You will likely additionally need to sell if the company has disposed of dividends since you won't win a standard paycheck from this stock any longer. In any case, on the off chance that you accept the company is as yet a strong speculation, it may be a decent time to buy considerably increasingly stock.

We hear "broadening" a great deal in the money related administrations industry. Expansion is, all in all, a time-tried and sound contributing strategy. Be that as it may, numerous investors commit the error of over-enhancement inside a

Dividend Investing

single sector. Basically, you will never need to claim multiple names from a particular industry. The least complex contributing strategy inside a sector is to buy the two best performing names in it. There's actually no motivation to possess anything else than that. Another common contributing misstep is buying names inside a sector carefully dependent on stock price. This is likely the most noticeably terrible approach to move toward a sector in light of the fact that the least expensive stocks inside a sector are never the best ones to possess. On most events, the substantially more costly stock will outperform the modest one. I would generally preferably possess 25 shares of a $200 stock over 1,000 shares of a $5 stock.

Talking about price, I like to be obtuse with regards to depicting "modest" stocks. Stocks are typically "modest" for an explanation, and most have earned those low prices with poor company performance. Buying modest stocks isn't being wise; it's being stupid! Investigate the performance of Warren Buffet's Berkshire Hathaway Class A (BRK-A) shares in Figures 5.5 and 5.6. You could have gotten one share at about $6,000 a share in the mid-1990s. Truth is stranger than fiction, $6,000 for one share. Sounds costly, correct? All things considered, those shares hit a high of $140,000 per share in 2008 and have since pulled back a piece. Same

The Importance Of Diversification

manage a tech mammoth, Google (GOOG), despite the fact that on a littler scale. Google appeared at almost $90 a share in 2004, which appeared to be costly at the time. By 2007, be that as it may, Google stock was worth more than $700 per share, in spite of the fact that it's pulled back altogether from those highs.

In outline, investors should buy the best stocks inside the sectors that are currently working, paying little respect to their share price. Simply recall, two stocks inside every sector is more than adequate for your portfolio.

Expansion is about more than buying different stocks. Similarly, as you shouldn't put all your money in a single company, you likewise shouldn't place all your money in a single industry. In the event that you do, and an issue hits that specific industry, you are probably going to suffer misfortunes to your whole stock portfolio. For instance, if another tax is reported on all medicinal services companies, the share prices of those companies are probably going to endure. Positively, you need to research each and every company you add to your stock portfolio. You should know, however much as could be expected about each stock you buy. Never buy a stock only for broadening. It is smarter to claim one stock that you are con scratch is a wise speculation than three if two of them are awful risks. Growing your portfolio will take some time. Go slowly and pick astutely.

Choosing High-Yield Stocks

You will most likely not foresee how well a particular company will do; however, you can place the chances in support of you by putting resources into specific sorts of companies. A few companies are almost certain than others to keep up a relentless ascension. These are likewise the companies that are probably going to pay you the most in dividends. Numerous individuals consider blue-chip stocks to be the best wagers for long-term dividend income. These companies are among the best in the nation; some are even the top companies on the planet. They got their name from blue poker chips, which have the highest estimation of the considerable number of hues. Many blue-chip companies are listed on the Dow Jones, Nasdaq, and S&P 500 indexes. Each of the thirty companies on the Dow pay dividends. A considerable lot of the companies on these lists are viewed as the best companies to put resources into if you need an unfaltering month to month or quarterly income. Furthermore, in light of the fact that they are a piece of major indexes, it is anything but difficult to follow the advancement of these stocks. Open any money related newspaper or website, and you will have

The Importance Of Diversification

the option to check the current price of your stock. The companies that are probably going to pay the highest yields are banks, utilities, royalty trusts, land venture trusts (REITs), and master limited partnerships (MLPs). Cautious determination is as yet an unquestionable requirement, particularly with regards to banks. Banks that are doing admirably can pay the absolute highest dividends in the stock market. Banks that have done ineffectively in the course of the most recent quite a long while, in any case, have made gigantic cuts to their dividends.

Utility companies are businesses that provide fundamental administrations, for example, power, gas, and water. In any event, when the economy is awful, individuals still need these administrations. Hence, utility companies, as a rule, perform superior to numerous different companies, even in difficult financial conditions. Utility stocks additionally tend to pay higher dividends than different stocks. Land speculation trusts work, particularly like different companies that offer stock to people in general. REITs bargain explicitly inland, notwithstanding. They buy, sell, and oversee different sorts of property or even home loans. You may think about these companies as huge scale landowners. REITs were first formed when the Real Estate Investment Trust Act went in 1960. The demonstration offered these

Dividend Investing

companies certain tax breaks. One of the states of fitting the bill for REIT status is that the company must apportion 90 percent of its net income to its shareholders.

Albeit a couple of REITs offer direct stock purchase plans, many don't, so shares of their companies must be purchased through an intermediary. Beside their high yields, perhaps the greatest bit of leeway of REITs is their price. A significant number of the trade for only $10 to $40 a share and offer dividend yields somewhere in the range of 3 and 12 percent.

Royalty trusts are like REITs, yet these companies bargain explicitly in land that is high in characteristic vitality sources, for example, oil. It's anything but tedious to perceive any reason why these investments are great ones at the present time. The rising costs of coal, oil, and gaseous petrol make royalty trusts ace table investments. Their dividends often pay somewhere in the range of 9 and 15 percent. Since royalty trusts pay such a great amount to their investors, however, consider a company's cash flow before contributing. In the case of things turns out badly, will the company have the option to continue paying such high dividends?

Master limited partnerships additionally share

The Importance Of Diversification

90 percent or a greater amount of their profits with the individuals who put resources into their companies. Investors in MLPs aren't called shareholders, however. Rather, they are limited partners in the companies. Likewise, the pieces of the company that these limited partners possess aren't shares; they are called units. As far as possible, the sorts of companies that can offer MLPs to their investors. You can typically detect a MLP by the letters "LP" toward the finish of the company's name. A large number of these businesses bargain in products and regular asset materials. Few them are money management rms. Master limited partnerships likewise don't utilize the term dividends. Rather, they pay out what they call quarterly required appropriations (QRDs). These payments work a great deal like dividends, yet there is one significant distinction. Master limited partnerships must make these payments to their investors.

The favorable position for the companies that qualify as master limited partnerships is that they pay no corporate income taxes. Consequently, MLPs generally offer a lot higher yields on their QRDs than most stock dividends pay. You likewise might have the option to pay lower taxes when you get your QRD payments; however, taxes could be higher than normal capital gains taxes when you sell. Ensured payouts and high yields are positive focal points. Yet, these advantages don't delete the risk of putting resources into any of these companies. In these cases, the risk becomes an integral factor when you think about how well a specific company performs. On the off chance that a company falls flat, 90 percent of its profits could be nothing by any means. Income stocks ought to be long-term investments. In a perfect world, you need to buy stock and keep it for a long time. Trading is always an alternative, obviously, and sometimes it must be done to restrict misfortunes. All in all, however, you need to buy stock in the companies that are well on the way to climate any monetary tempests they may experience.

Developing Your Stock Portfolio

When you make a stock portfolio, you will, at that point, need to oversee it. By what means will you choose which stocks to add to your portfolio? What number of offers will you buy? In what capacity will you choose when to sell the ventures that aren't working for you just as you had trusted? Your responses to these inquiries might be altogether different from those of another financial specialist. As another financial specialist, you will need to keep your risk as low as conceivable until you have more understanding. You additionally might not have

The Importance Of Diversification

as a lot of cash as you might want when you initially begin. By settling on brilliant choices now, however, you will ideally have more money to contribute later. To make the greater part of the money you do have, search for the stocks that offer steady dividends.

Obviously, consistent dividends aren't generally the most noteworthy dividends. You might need to devote a level of your portfolio to the blue-chip companies that offer the most significant returns. Regardless of whether you start with the thirty distinctive Dow stocks, you can undoubtedly recognize the five or ten companies that pay the most in dividends. A few speculators buy just these stocks. In a year, they may even sell any stocks that have dropped o¬ this rundown, supplanting them with the companies that have had their spot in the best ten. You ought to never buy a stock dependent on yield alone, however. Make certain to investigate an organization's history, accounts, and the board altogether before you contribute.

Suppose you have $1,000 to begin your stock portfolio. You may choose to partition your money similarly between two stocks, buying $500 worth of offers in each organization. Another alternative would place more money into the stock that pays the better return. Maybe you would put $750 in that stock and $250 in the other. You could even choose three stocks. For this situation, you could put $333.33 in each organization, or $500 in one and $250 in every one of the other two. For whatever length of time that you fulfill the base buy sums, you can isolate your underlying speculation any way you choose. As you have more money to contribute, you might need to enhance further to decrease your hazard.

Regardless of whether you have enough money to buy your stock altogether, you may, at present, consider paying a month to month sum for an immediate stock buy plan. This technique, called dollar-cost averaging, is another way you can diminish your hazard. Assume you buy $500 worth of stock today in an organization whose offers are selling for $25 each. Possibly you have gotten your work done and are con mark that the stock will pay you ordinary dividends and furthermore go up in an incentive throughout the following five years. Presently assume that the stock drops by $5 per share one month from now, and drops again by another $5 the next month. Your venture may even now go up in an incentive after some time, however, for right now, you have lost money, $200 to be precise. On the event that you had contributed $50 month to month rather, you would have more money accessible to buy more offers when the value dropped. You would have likewise lost

The Importance Of Diversification

less money when the stock value fell. Obviously, in the event that the cost had expanded as you expected, at that point, your later buys would have been made at those more significant expenses.

On the off chance that you have low maintenance work, you may choose to put resources into a few distinctive DSPPs. In the event that you choose companies that have least month to month measures of just $25, these ventures would just cost you $75 every month. If you think about how a lot of cash you will make back in dividends, your month to month speculation is even less. Provided that you need to make much more, you could try out the companies' profit reinvestment programs—a far and away superior approach to exploit dollar-cost averaging. Regardless of what your own profit stock technique is, make careful research a customary piece of any stock buy you make. When you have picked an organization, set out to find out about it wherever you can. What's more, remember to find out about the challenge. Tune in to what your folks and companions need to state about the organization also, particularly on the off chance that they are clients of the organization or another like it. Sometimes it doesn't take a money related master to distinguish a blemish in a specific organization. Indeed, even

Dividend Investing

companies that were once pioneers in their enterprises can make exorbitant slip-ups and end up useless.

Take, for instance, the account of Eastman Kodak. In 1888, Eastman Kodak presented a camera that was not normal for any camera that had preceded it. With the trademark "you press the catch, we wrap up," Kodak meant to make photography available to the regular customer. Kodak kept on advancing, making cameras simpler to utilize and film simpler to create. By 1930, Eastman Kodak was a blue-chip company recorded on the Dow Jones Industrial Average. Through the mid-1990s, the stock paid consistently expanding dividends.

Kodak's plan of action concentrated on selling lm, not cameras. Film was less expensive to create, all the more expert table, and consumable—so customers would buy it again and again. Cameras were purchased substantially less frequently. Be that as it may, the computerized age was starting to come to fruition, and lm was rapidly getting out of date. The company that once came out on top in development was, in effect, gradually pushed out of the market by different companies that were making progresses with new technology. A few investigators recommend that Kodak's administration had gotten careless, depending

The Importance Of Diversification

on the company's past progress and notoriety, as opposed to searching out new thoughts. In the meantime, contenders kept on making more up to date and better items.

In 1994, Kodak announced its first profit cut, keeping extra money in its financial balance to put resources into creating computerized technology. Another CEO was procured to bring Kodak into the cutting edge age. It appeared that Kodak was keeping pace with the business, and it's stock value moved to a high of $94.75 in 1997. Shockingly, Kodak's e¬ orts to change were short of what was expected. By 2003, the company had to cut dividends once more, and in 2004 the stock was expelled from the Dow. In 2009, dividends were dispensed with totally and offer costs sunk to $2.01.

As a component of its 2012 liquidation ling, Kodak announced another business structure proposed to bring the company and its items into the twenty-first century. It is not yet clear, in any case, regardless of whether Kodak can reappear as an effective company by and by. In a quickly evolving world, instances of once-solid companies incapable to keep up are anything but difficult to discover. The downturn that started in 2007 featured shortcomings in numerous companies, particularly banks. Because of the money related emergency, Bank

Dividend Investing

of America had to cut its yearly dividends from $2.24 in 2008 to simply $0.04 the next year. Offers that had exchanged as high as $45.08 in 2008 exchanged at a low of $2.53 in 2009. In spite of the fact that offer costs have expanded from that point forward, they presently can't seem to completely recuperate, and dividends are still low.

Different stocks that were once viewed as development stocks have developed into stable profit stocks. Companies like Microsoft and Intel were on the front line of technology when they were shaped. Today, they are commonly recognized names that numerous experts consider to be wise speculations. In any case, on the off chance that they don't stay aware of their rivals, even these companies could wind up bankrupt. While numerous individuals get their recommendation from experienced investigators, even these "specialists" commit errors. Youngsters might be at a preferred position in picking solid stocks for the future since they are frequently progressively mindful of changes that are going on in the enterprises that they like. Numerous renowned financial specialists suggest "purchasing what you know"— or building a stock portfolio of companies whose items and administrations you really use. As a customer, you recognize what you like and what you don't. With a little research, you might have the option to recognize which companies' arrangements are probably going to be effective later on, and which ones are starting to fall antiquated.

In any case, it is shrewd to keep your feelings out of your stock portfolio. Maybe you might want to possess stock in your preferred café or garments company. On the off chance that the examination bolsters the plan to put resources into this company, there is unquestionably nothing amiss with doing as such, as long as you let the numbers control your choices.

When to Sell a Dividend Stock

Very much an excess of consideration is given to buying stocks and insufficient to when it is suitable to sell. Also, there are times during a financial specialist's lifetime when it will bode well to lessen or maybe even totally sell out of a dividend stock portfolio. Stocks become exaggerated, and bear markets hit, by and large, every five or six years. In the previous 60 years, we have had eleven bear markets, and I envision this pace of recurrence will proceed. In a perfect world, one ensures capital just as conceivable during these draw-downs – which means selling stocks.

At the point when you choose to sell a dividend

stock, it includes a choice to sell, however another, maybe similarly troublesome choice of what to buy with the proceeds of the sale. Along these lines, preceding making a sale, you ought to likewise have a smart thought concerning what you expect to do with the proceeds. Of course, maybe you will utilize the money to help spread certain every day costs or different needs, however on the off chance that not, you'll need an arrangement set up before the sale. Hence, knowing why you are selling and what you are going to buy a while later, entangle matters, selling in an assessable record can include a taxation rate (capital additions charges might be expected) so one must know about the duty consequences of a sale, the amount you may possibly owe the administration (accepting you can't counterbalance the increase with a misfortune in a similar expense year), and consider the duties before pulling the trigger on the sale. Primary concern, I have discovered that most investors experience more difficulty selling than buying. In the event that you include the enthusiastic connection that a few investors may feel for specific organizations that have treated them well throughout the years, it can make going separate ways, paying little mind to valuations and dangers about outlandish.

There are numerous legitimate purposes behind

The Importance Of Diversification

selling a dividend stock, and we'll take a gander at some of them in this area.

Reasons to sell a dividend stock:

- Stocks are exaggerated. There are times when the whole stock market can become exaggerated to such a degree, that it makes sense to reduce stock situations to secure riches. The market truly exchanges at a CAPE ratio (consistently balanced cost to income) of around 16.5. Typically it will exchange a genuinely tight range around this valuation; however, given the cyclicality of the business sectors and the irrational conduct of members, markets will now and then exchange a long way past ordinary estimating. At the point when valuations ascend to risky levels, it frequently makes sense to sell stocks just to secure your capital. This has nothing to do with your opinion of the possibilities of a specific organization in your portfolio – it is progressively an acknowledgment that the whole market is exaggerated to such an extent, that all stocks become powerless against a remedy or bear showcase. Since times of high valuation are frequently trailed by underneath normal or negative returns, my conviction is that if the stock market has been in a bullish mode for a specific number of years (maybe four or five years into a recuperation) and supposition is sure and valuations gotten over the top, it is ideal to reduce risk. What's more, the best way to reduce risk might be to sell a portion of your dividend stock possessions. As a general guideline, I would consider a CAPE ratio more than 20 as a notice sign and, at any rate, think about diminishing risk by then.

- The dividend is reduced or at risk of being reduced or dispensed with. 2008-09 was a period when numerous money related organizations were broke, and income was plunging. To me, clearly, numerous organizations were not going to have the option to support their dividends – even organizations that had recently paid dividends reliably for a considerable length of time started lessening or taking out dividends. This is a valid justification to sell a stock. Sadly, when the updates on a dividend cut are declared, it is frequently as of now calculated into the cost of the stock, and it has most likely previously dropped a lot fully expecting the news. Along these

The Importance Of Diversification

lines, so as to secure yourself, you need to be in front of the group and attempt to make sense of whether an organization you claim is at risk of a dividend cut. Watch out for dividend growth, profit projections, the payout ratio and the money position of the organization to decide whether the dividend might be at risk. Worth Line stock reports show a decent depiction of the balance sheet of an organization, and you can see the money accessible, payout ratio and the dividend and income growth of the earlier 10 years. The reports likewise show projections for the coming a very long time for income and dividend growth, which can assist you with surveying risk. Expecting you comprehend the matter of the organization you possess, you ought to have a decent understanding concerning whether the dividend will be at risk (ideally never). In the event that you are concerned and you are scrutinizing the supportability of the dividend, my proposal is to sell as opposed to risk the stock value being whacked when a cut is at long last declared.

- The dividend payout ratio arrives at an unsustainable level. The dividend payout ratio is the dividend per offer partitioned by the profit per share, communicated as a ratio. Expecting an organization is built up and wins steady benefits; it might be the objective of the top managerial staff to attempt to keep up a certain payout ratio after some time. In this way, as the organization develops its income per share, it will likewise expand the dividend payout to investors. In any case, in the event that a payout gets excessively high and surpasses profit, at that point, the dividend will be at risk. Indeed, money on the balance sheet can be utilized to incidentally continue a dividend, yet in the long run, the dividend must be paid from income. Watch out for the current payout ratio and the historical backdrop of the payout ratio, as well. Once more, most organizations will attempt to keep up a certain payout ratio – you can discover the historical backdrop of the payout ratio through Value Line or numerous other money-related Web destinations. For instance, both PepsiCo and Coca-Cola have attempted to keep up payout ratios around half over the previous decade. Chevron and Exxon Mobil have ordinarily had payout ratios around 30%, and Johnson and Johnson return about 40% of its income as dividends to

The Importance Of Diversification

investors. In the event that you see an example where the payout ratio is expanding because of maybe income declining or the organization is developing its dividend all the more gradually, you should regard this as a warning and think about a closeout of the stock. Likewise, recollect that specific ventures customarily have higher payout ratios than others – telecom and utilities payout ratio ought to have a past filled with being at a genuinely predictable level, on account of a liberal governing body and steady profit and dividend growth.

- A stock position gets overweight in your portfolio. On the off chance that a stock you claim has acknowledged to such a degree that it becomes exaggerated, yet it additionally turns out to be vigorously weighted in your portfolio, you ought to think about decreasing the size of the holding. Conventional portfolio the board would propose an individual position ought not to be bigger than 6% of your all-out portfolio. On the event that you have a place that may be begun at this level and has developed to 10% or more, certainly consider a deal to reduce single-stock risk and further broaden your possessions.

Dividend Investing

- The consolidated dividend yield and dividend growth are ugly comparative with securities. In spite of the fact that it has been numerous years since this was the situation, there have been periods in history where it is difficult to legitimize owning dividend stocks if securities are paying rates that are alluring. Bonds are generally substantially less risky than stocks and, furthermore, don't have about the unpredictability of stocks, so in a situation where you can get enough intrigue salary from a bond portfolio, why claim dividend stocks? Lamentably in the present low-yield condition, security yields will most likely not be appealing comparative with dividend yields for a long time to come. Be that as it may, if middle of the road term speculation level corporate securities yield in the 4% to 6% territory, expansion is in line, and stocks are either genuinely esteemed or exaggerated, I unquestionably think it makes sense to sell in any event a bit of your dividend stocks to broaden and catch an appealing yield in a less unpredictable and less risky resource class – securities.

- The organization's stock value starts to encounter more volatility than before, and you are uncomfortable. The

The Importance Of Diversification

proportion of a stock's value volatility comparative with the market itself is characterized as beta. I regularly incline toward stocks that have low volatility, a beta around 40% not exactly the market itself, or 0.60. In any case, realize that beta is in reverse looking, and it is difficult to know without a doubt what's in store similar to the volatility of a specific holding. All things considered, in the event that you track the value development of the stocks you claim decently closely, you might have the option to recognize examples of volatility comparative with the market and on the off chance that you see one of your holdings is displaying more volatility than you foreseen and it is making you uncomfortable, think about a deal. Why keep on clutching a stock on the off chance that it is more unpredictable than the market, and its beta has expanded as of late (after your unique buy) to where it's creation you uncomfortable? In the event that you can locate an elective dividend stock that meets your criteria and is less unpredictable, at that point by all methods considering swapping out and lessening the volatility of your portfolio.

- There are other dividend stocks you

would prefer to claim. Now and again, you might be completely put resources into dividend stocks in your portfolio, and a stock you don't possess yet have had your eye on decreases to an alluring level. In the event that the general market is in a bullish pattern and valuations are sensible, and a stock on your watch rundown decays, it's likely a result of an acquiring's notice or decreased viewpoint by the organization. Expecting the gaining's "miss" is transitory, this can give a chance to you to sell one of your current holdings in the event that you accept your money will work better somewhere else. On the event that you can get a superior dividend yield and higher dividend development with an alternate organization that you would prefer to claim, at that point, think about making a move. You need the best return joined with reliable and supportable dividend development in an organization, and if you have a superior contender for your portfolio than one of your current positions, at that point, you ought to surely think about a swap.

- You lose faith in the organization – out of the blue. I don't have a specific connection to any stock, and neither

The Importance Of Diversification

should you. I attempt my best to evacuate my feelings to settle on the levelheaded portfolio the executive's choices. Sooner or later, in dealing with your portfolio (most likely when you are losing money), you will, without a doubt, question huge numbers of your holdings, or you may lose faith in the path an organization is taking. You may scrutinize its choice to present a specific item or make an interest in a specific industry. These are unquestionably reasons to audit why you claim an organization, and on the off chance that you are not persuaded, you need to possess it at the present value; at that point, you ought to think about a deal.

- You have personal financial reasons to sell. You truly shouldn't have money put resources into any dividend stock or the market itself on the off chance that you are going to require that money in the following a few years. The purpose behind this is clear since nobody can anticipate with extraordinary conviction what stock costs will do at whatever year, and with a period skyline of just a couple of years, there is chance that your money won't be there when you need it. Along these lines, on the off chance that you realize you are going to require a specific dollar measure of your portfolio for up and coming costs in the following scarcely any years, it might be shrewd to decrease chance sooner than later and raise money currently by selling shares. You would prefer not to chance school educational cost, an upfront installment on your fantasy home, or some other basic cost you can't forego that is coming up in the following not many years. Start lessening danger well ahead of time of a forthcoming commitment by selling a portion of your dividend stocks fully expecting requiring the money for personal financial reasons.

Main concern, regardless of whether you are a purchase and-hold speculator, that doesn't mean you should purchase and-overlook. You should watch out for the entirety of your holdings, and there are not very many stocks, assuming any, that can be held until the end of time. Evacuate your feelings – each stock is a possibility for a deal at some level.

HOW TO MANAGE YOUR PORTFOLIO TO CONTROL RISK

So as to manage your portfolio well to control risk, you have to give specific consideration to where we are in any monetary cycle, bull or bear market, and in particular, what current valuations are demonstrating about future projected returns. Risk can be characterized as the vulnerability of future returns and the probability of capital misfortune, maybe perpetual misfortune. This is the risk that financial specialists care about most. Most "proficient" financial specialists and academicians characterize risk as the unpredictability of returns; however, I would differ, and I accept that the main risks we genuinely care about are the vulnerability of future returns and the risk of misfortune.

Perceiving risk starts with a comprehension of significant worth and knowing when an asset is estimated high comparative with the projected return. Thus, high risk with a low projected return is obviously an affirmation of the connection among worth and cost and the related risk.

Dividend Investing

Risks increment as markets and valuations ascend, since the projected and anticipated returns, in view of verifiable valuations and value patterns, decrease. Simply, as a positively trending market ages and prices rise, financial specialists become more risk-accommodating, searching for more prominent returns, despite the fact that history would propose the contrary will happen. At the point when financial specialists are eager to accept more risk, because of maybe ongoing positive returns on account of rising prices, the objective speculator ought to be suspicious of future positive returns proceeding at a similar pace. Also, on the off chance that you will accept the risk, don't you need similar potential returns for expecting the risk? Things being what they are, the cause would the apathetic, prudent financial specialist buy even more a stock or resource class as it gets pricier and the projected return decays? It doesn't bode well, yet this is the means by which the vast majority of the contributing open carries on.

At the point when speculators have scarcely any stresses and are self-satisfied, frequently in light of the fact that ongoing returns have been relentless and positive, they build up a resilience for risk and pay more significant expenses for resources. During times of high valuations or air pockets, as cost-to-income products rise, low or even negative projected returns become likely in future years. Along these lines, it's basic to perceive when risks are raised and projected returns become ugly. The level of risk present in the market is dictated by the behavior of the members (buyers and dealers), and whenever overlooked, will prompt perhaps poor returns and unquestionably ugly returns on a risk-balanced premise. At limits, avarice and the probability of income sans work and benefits urge the crowd to heap into speculations with little respect for risk, esteem, or a comprehension of the results of their activities. This is the thing that pushes markets into perilous air pocket an area. It likewise comes from a conviction that the great occasions will proceed, uncertainly, and expanded risk isn't really viewed as expanded at the time it is accepted. At the end of the day, the unreasonable, commonplace speculator doesn't perceive that risks have risen – the person accepts the venture is generally safe and has been adapted to accept so by the appealing late returns. All in all, if that isn't generally risky, why not buy more?

Most speculators are ignorant that their behavior and consequent value moves cause market risk to rise and fall. Absolutely risks ascend as they collect more resources (stocks and land), and the inverse is valid on the off chance that they are emptying resources in a frenzy (bear market behavior) – the market really turns out to be less risky as future returns look progressively appealing. The expanded certainty of the retail financial specialist and even the "proficient" support director should make the more profound scholar stressed as projected returns are scaled-down because of rising prices. What's more, the inverse is genuine, as well. In the event that financial specialists are of the mentality that "I won't buy that at any value, it's excessively risky," there may be an extraordinary chance to benefit for the individuals who can remember it. On the off chance that everybody accepts a venture is risky, it most likely isn't, actually, since, at a discouraged value, future returns are presumably very good. Also, obviously, if everybody accepts that risk is low and future appealing returns are likely, the more prepared speculator will presumably decide the inverse is bound to happen. To put it plainly, what is of most extreme significance in understanding the connection between value, worth, and risk is that the value paid for an advantage and the projected future returns will extraordinarily decide the degree of risk.

A decent financial specialist can control risk, most importantly, on the grounds that the individual in question remembers it exists and has an understanding when it is raised. In any case, since there are more great years than terrible in the financial exchange, this acknowledgment of risk may just get clear in awful years (negative market returns) – that risk control was significant and essential at the time. Risk control fully expecting a bear market or rectification is basic, and the goal of losing not exactly the market itself and limiting drawdowns is a commendable interest. Or then again, if conceivable, to not lose any cash would be perfect.

The main concern is it is a venture director's business to wisely accept risk for potential benefit when it bodes well. We can accept risk when the reward is advantageous. We can never stay away from risk through and through, since the future is mysterious, yet we can put forth a valiant effort to control it and even welcome it now and again.

Proposed strategy to help control risk:

Reduce beta

On the off chance that we concur that the vulnerability of future returns and the probability of misfortune are the risks we care about most, at that point clearly when markets are exaggerated on a chronicled premise and

Dividend Investing

future anticipated returns are extremely low or even negative, this is the point at which we have to make changes in accordance with a portfolio to control risk. Sometimes you may need to reduce the beta of your portfolios by some rate say 20-30%. This is an initial step you can do to control risk in the event that you accept markets are exaggerated. Keep in mind; beta is a proportion of instability for a stock or a whole portfolio comparative with the market itself. In a low-beta portfolio (for example, 0.60), accepting history rehashes itself, you would lose 60% of the sum that the market would lose in a downtrend. For instance, if the market drops 10%, with a low-beta portfolio of 0.60, your portfolio would decay by just 6%. Reducing beta in your portfolio is a decent initial step to controlling risk. The long haul normal CAPE ratio for stocks is 16.5, so if stocks are exchanging over that level, you could think about bringing down risk in your portfolio by reducing beta or by selling stocks.

In the event that you focus on the CAPE ratio and it is raised (20 or above), and future returns look beneath normal, you may choose to not just reduce beta in your current stock property, you may likewise choose to reduce risk by selling a part of your portfolio and raising cash or moving into momentary bonds. Truly, you could be surrendering potential future gains thusly;

How To Manage Your Portfolio To Control Risk

however, you will likewise secure riches and the benefits you have amassed.

Reduce stock presentation

As a buyer market ages and valuations rise, you can control risk by stripping and selling down your stock property. You could begin, for instance, by reducing your stock portfolio by maybe a quarter or a third, if valuations surpass 20 on the CAPE ratio. In the event that we climb to 22 or 25, you could sell another third or even a higher rate. As we moved higher and anticipated returns are reduced, you would raise cash and securing your benefits and your riches. This seems like presence of mind, yet it is especially hard to do when it appears as though gains come so effectively and there is little motivation to stress (average late positively trending market conduct). Indeed, you may choose to "let it ride" for some time, yet sooner or later, the additions could vanish immediately when patterns turn around, so it is basic that you have a game plan set up to reduce risk.

Admonition – many purchase and-hold fans accept they can claim a portfolio of top-notch organizations perpetually, absent a lot of risk of misfortune, either impermanent or changeless. They accept that owning incredible profit payers or organizations that sell items that are popular paying little heed to the quality of the economy, is constantly worth holding. I oppose this idea. Quality resources become risky if the value paid is too high, and the future return of the "quality" resource is excessively low or even negative. Everything relies upon the value you pay (it decides quality), and there is no doubt as far as I can tell that we regularly overpay for what are seen as quality organizations at any value – and many are uninformed of the risks of acquiring at raised costs. Keep in mind; many "excellent" stocks sell at high products and costs since they are thought to be such spectacular speculations and merit a superior cost. Nonetheless, kindly perceive that in the midst of outrageous overvaluation or air pockets, it doesn't make a difference how much "quality" you have in your portfolio – these stocks can get clobbered as well.

I would be fast to agree that dealing with a portfolio to control risk is more craftsmanship than science – that is the thing that makes it so troublesome. You can control risk by reducing beta, and you can likewise control risk by selling stocks as the market moves past authentic reasonable worth and well into an exaggerated area. These are the two essential ways you can control risk, yet you should initially perceive when risks are raised. A wary way to deal with contributing bodes well for about everybody and absolutely for retirees or those approaching retirement. In the event that you attempt to control risk and stay away from awful bear-market misfortunes, your returns can, at present, be awesome and reliable enough to enable you to be monetarily agreeable for an amazing duration. Indeed, you may pass up some energy toward the finish of a super positively trending market, yet on the off chance that you contribute protectively and limit draw-downs at whatever point conceivable, you stand a magnificent possibility of accomplishing your speculation objectives.

STRATEGIES FOR SAFE PORTFOLIO WITHDRAWALS

Safe withdrawal rates in retirement and strategies for proper withdrawals, as a level of the estimation of one's portfolio, are seldom examined, especially during bullish times when most investors are going through as they wish with little worry about draining their assets. The purpose behind this is investors pull back cash from their portfolios to cover costs, maybe at irrational rates of 6% or higher every year, yet their portfolios still keep on developing every year during a positively trending market, which enables them to overlook what could turn into a major issue when the following bear market hits and they are reluctant or incapable to reduce their spending.

In this segment, we'll audit different strategies for safe withdrawals and probabilities of accomplishment with various asset allocations. We will likewise take a gander at what I accept is of most extreme significance at this specific time – fitting rates of withdrawals in a low-yield security market and profoundly esteemed financial exchange.

Overviews have more than once demonstrated

Strategies For Safe Portfolio Withdrawals

that retirees and those approaching retirement have little thought regarding how a lot of cash they can pull back from their portfolios in retirement and still not outlast their cash. Over 70% of Americans have not, in any case, known about the purported 4% withdrawal principle, which is the standard in the business for what ought to be a rule for sensible yearly withdrawals in retirement. Numerous retirees think a withdrawal rate of 6% to 8% is sensible and practical, in spite of the realities talking boisterously despite what might be expected. Along these lines, there is a lot of the American open ought to find out about this theme as most are ill-equipped and ineffectively educated.

Clearly, the objective for most investors is to grow a portfolio to a specific level preceding retirement (by sparing and contributing) with the goal that they would then be able to begin to easily live off the portfolio all through retirement. Preferably, one would live off a portion of the pay and not contact the head. The objective is clearly to not outlast your cash and maybe additionally have a lot of assets to pass on to the people to come.

The initial phase in this procedure ought to be to decide the amount you figure you will spend in retirement on a yearly premise. Start with the rudiments and include your costs for the coming

Dividend Investing

year and afterward subtract that number from any pay you are accepting outside of your portfolio – social security, annuity installments, benefits, rental salary, and so on. Whatever amount that remaining parts is the amount that should be pulled back from your venture portfolio to keep up your lifestyle. The absolute dollar amount to be pulled back every year will be your spending rate or withdrawal rate – a specific level of your portfolio's worth. Truly, it can differ after some time, yet it is critical, to begin with, a sensible withdrawal rate and attempt to factor in your time horizon, asset allocation, and above all, your life expectancy. On the event that you are a couple, your time horizon will be the life expectancy of the enduring mate. For most, there is a decent possibility your retirement assets should most recent 20 years or more.

Here's a straightforward case of a retiree who has yearly pay needs of $80,000 and a $1.5 million portfolio. This retiree gets $1,000 every month in social security and an extra $2,000 in month to month benefits salary or around $36,000 yearly. Along these lines, there is a deficit of $44,000 every year. Accepting this retiree at that point pulls back $44,000 from the portfolio every year, the withdrawal rate is 2.93%.

4% Rule

The 4% safe withdrawal rate was promoted by monetary organizer William Bengen in 1994 and was additionally best in class by the Trinity Study in 1998. The examinations fundamentally show that most portfolio blends of stocks and securities in retirement, paying little heed to the rate put resources into every asset class, and accepting a retirement as long as 30 years, will be fruitful with a withdrawal rate at 4% every year. By "achievement," I mean the financial specialist doesn't outlast the portfolio. The examinations further factor in a yearly expansion change, so one's dollar withdrawal amount builds every year to stay aware of the rate of swelling. In its least complex structure, utilizing the 4% rule, the retiree would ascertain 4% of the closure portfolio balance at whatever year to decide the most extreme dollar amount to be pulled back in the ensuing year. The dollar dispersion can emerge out of profit salary, security premium, or sadly, from selling a few property – this includes assaulting head, which is vital if pay is low or potentially your withdrawal rate is excessively high.

As I would see it, the issue with applying the 4% decide today is that the anticipated return suppositions utilized in the examinations done during the 1990s are extremely idealistic.

Dividend Investing

Normal yearly security returns of 5.5% and financial exchange returns of 10% every year won't emerge in the coming years. How right? We have middle term securities paying around 1% every prior year charges, and there is essentially no upside potential for capital additions with securities since rates are at wretchedly low levels. Simply, as I would like to think, portfolio returns from any blend of stocks and bonds in the coming years will miss the mark regarding verifiable normal returns, and this introduces an undeniable test for investors resigning now or anybody living off a portfolio with a life expectancy of 15 years or more.

Furthermore, I will contend that retirees with a time horizon of 30 years or longer ought to pull back far under 4% every year from a portfolio (maybe a large portion of that amount would be perfect) so as to guarantee a portfolio endures. As the retiree ages and life expectancy diminishes, one could consider knocking up the withdrawal rate above 4%, yet 4% truly is certifiably not a protected rate for most in the present condition. In any case, if you take a gander at the portfolio achievement insights in the Ibbotson information, it shows up as though you don't have anything to stress over accepting you adhere to the 4% rate, paying little heed to your asset allocation. Once more, I oppose this idea.

Strategies For Safe Portfolio Withdrawals

While many people have, for quite some time, been a defender of the 4% rule and have exhorted their clients to utilize it as a rule previously, I never again trust it is a protected withdrawal rate given current low yields. Here are a few recommendations I need to put the chances all the more exceptionally in support of you for a monetarily agreeable retirement:

• Don't increase your withdrawal rate every year to keep pace with expansion. For example, if you begin your withdrawal rate at 4% at age 70, stay with the 4% rate and don't increase your withdrawal rate every year to stay aware of swelling.

- Reduce your withdrawal rate during adjustments or bear markets. On the off chance that your portfolio has declined 10% to 20% or more, reduce the sum you pull back, so you have the most obvious opportunity to recuperate misfortunes when the market, in the long run, turns bullish once more. Once more, I prompt decreasing your withdrawal rate when your portfolio performs ineffectively. For instance, if your portfolio is down 10% in the earlier year, maybe curtailing your withdrawal rate to 3% or less would be proper since this would mean you have more money in your portfolio to ideally recover when stocks in the long run recoup. The issue with this strategy, obviously, is that numerous retirees can't or reluctant to curtail during intense markets or during any market environment besides. On the off chance that one keeps on pulling back 4% or more during a drawn-out bear market of quite a while or more, there is an extraordinary danger of coming up short on money, and the portfolio may lose esteem (lackluster showing and high withdrawals) a lot quicker than foreseen. Once more, I lean toward a financial specialist be in a situation to change withdrawal rates to market conditions.

- Cut your costs and reduce your withdrawal rate to underneath 4% if your life expectancy is past 15 years. On the off chance that your life expectancy is past 15 years, and especially in the present low-yield environment, you hazard incredibly exhausting your portfolio, even at a 4% withdrawal rate. For anybody with a life expectancy or time skyline past 15 years, consider lessening your withdrawals to under 3% every year to give your portfolio a superior opportunity to get by in any market environment. On the off chance

Strategies For Safe Portfolio Withdrawals

that loan fees in the long run come back to increasingly typical levels and additionally stocks fall enough to where the anticipated returns become progressively appealing, at that point you could increase your withdrawals to the 4% territory or higher, however until that happens my proposal is to be reasonable and bring down your withdrawals however much as could be expected.

Portfolio withdrawals in a low-yield environment

The research division at Morningstar has delivered some brilliant work on withdrawal rates that are as of now unmistakably more proper than crafted by the Bengen and Trinity Studies done during the 1990s. I would prescribe all financial specialists, especially those in or approaching retirement, read the investigations entirely on the Morningstar Web webpage. David Blanchett, Michael Finke, and Wade Pfau composed a paper in 2013 titled Low Bond Yields and Safe Withdrawal Rates that ought to be an eye-opener for retirees. This study, as I would like to think, is significantly more relevant in today's low-yield environment and factors in increasingly reasonable returns and furthermore expect a yearly speculation

Dividend Investing

warning charge of 1% - which is an average expense paid for portfolio the executives. The consequences of the study are amazing, calming and ought to be a reminder for all speculators.

Blanchett, Finke, and Pfau found in 2013 that while the first 4% rule promoted by Bengen in 1994 was satisfactory at the time, with financing costs now at truly low levels, and expenses and progressively sensible stock returns figured in, the 4% rule is in reality awfully forceful and much of the time just gives a half possibility of accomplishment. I don't care for those chances, and neither should you. I happen to concur with the Morningstar study, and when taken a gander at related to its magnificent study that components in equity valuations (surveyed in a minute), it should cause considerably more concern.

We should take a gander at a few models, utilizing Morningstar's information from 2013, for withdrawal rates with a low yield of 2% and a CAPE ratio of 22. I trust the portfolio's poor achievement rate adequately alarms you into pulling backless from your portfolio. Utilizing a 60% equity allocation (the equalization would be in securities) with retirement periods running from 15 to 35 years, one can perceive what the proper withdrawal rate ought to be for a foreordained achievement rate %. Today the security yield is still at a similar level as in 2013, yet the CAPE ratio is presently more like 27, so these equivalent projections would be even less idealistic whenever run today. Anyway, a retiree who needs a 90% likelihood of achievement over a 20-year retirement period, could pull back 3.7% every year. On the off chance that a similar retiree required to knock up the achievement rate to 99%, the fitting withdrawal rate should drop to 2.4% every year. Once more, this is utilizing information for a 20-year retirement and a 60% equity allocation.

Another case of a more youthful retiree who needs a 95% achievement rate % over a 30-year retirement shows a withdrawal rate of just 2.0% every year to be fitting. In the event that she pulls back 4.2%, she only has a half possibility of progress.

My point in referring to the more sensible projections set forth by Morningstar is an endeavor to persuade all financial specialists to reexamine current withdrawal rates, given our low-yield environment where 2% returns or less from securities are the standard, and to ideally persuade you to lower your withdrawal rate before it is past the point of no return. Once more, the first examinations from the 1990s are never again legitimate in the immediate environment. Proper withdrawal rates ought to really be about half lower than initially decided for retirements that may most recent 30 years or more. What's more, on the off chance that you choose not to cause a change in accordance with (lessen your withdrawals), realize that your chances of accomplishment are incredibly decreased in this low-yield environment.

Portfolio withdrawals in a low-yield and high valuation environment

In April 2013, the Morningstar inquire about trio of David Blanchett, Michael Finke, and Wade Pfau set forth a comprehensive study that took a gander at safe withdrawal rates when considering in low yielding bonds and stock market valuations. The paper titled Asset Valuations and Safe Portfolio Withdrawal Rates ought to be required perusing for all pre-retirees, retirees, and their counsels. As you are no uncertainty mindful, bond yields are at generally low levels, and stock market valuations are grand. As of February 2015, with a 10-year Treasury yield of 2.0% and a CAPE ratio of 27, we basically don't have any similar period in history to anticipate portfolio endurance rates – we are in an unchartered area. The investigations directed during the 1990s on portfolio survivability didn't factor in low financing costs or stock valuations, so Morningstar's study was long past due. At the

Strategies For Safe Portfolio Withdrawals

hour of the survey in 2013, the CAPE ratio was at 22, and the bond yield was at 2.0%.

Right now, almost two years after the fact, with a considerably higher stock market valuation and comparable bond yields, one would envision future achievement rates to be even lower than the rates found by Morningstar. What Messrs. Blanchett, Finke, and Pfau found was that withdrawal rates in a low yield bond condition, and a profoundly esteemed stock market should be a lot of lower than recently suspected to succeed. In the event that we utilize the 2% rate now accessible in a 10-year Treasury bond and a portfolio with a 60% value distribution, and a CAPE ratio perusing of 25, there is just a 48.5% possibility of progress for a retiree pulling back 4% every year from a portfolio. The entirety of the information expects a 4% withdrawal rate and a 30-year retirement.

Another model, utilizing the 40% value allotment table and a 2% bond yield with a CAPE ratio of 25, shows that if the financial specialist pulls back 4% every year over a 30-year retirement, he just has a 41.6% possibility of accomplishment.

Unmistakably, with a high CAPE ratio and a low bond yield, it is likely a retiree's portfolio won't

Dividend Investing

endure if withdrawal rates are excessively steep. To be sure, generally, low bond yields joined with verifiably high stock valuations have put numerous retirement portfolios in danger of being purged over the coming decades. I trust these examinations and my alerts persuade you to alter your withdrawal rate depending on current bond yields and value valuations. In taking a gander at the ongoing Morningstar study, and the information in the tables, you can obviously observe that paying little mind to your value allotment (20% to 80% values), in the event that you pull back over 4% every year and you are attempting to make your portfolio last 25 or 30 years, you will likely come up short. A 25-year retirement with an underlying 4% withdrawal rate, a 2% bond yield, and a 25 CAPE ratio have just a 50.2% possibility of progress (80% values). The outcomes are educational and discouraging.

In synopsis, in the event that one examination the relationship of profits and achievement rates between bond yields and portfolio withdrawal rates, one can oversee desires stock market valuations and costs appropriately. Meager bond yields and high stock valuations recommend that so as to make progress contributing, especially in retirement, one must decrease portfolio withdrawals drastically to improve the chances. For financial specialists with a retirement time skyline of 15 years or more, my recommendation is to diminish withdrawal rates by half of what you have become used to (maybe to 2.5% or less every year), and to oversee chance just as conceivable to ideally limit loss of head and secure capital during down years. It is essential to focus on and change your advantage designation and your withdrawal rate depending on the present market condition.

www.ingramcontent.com/pod-product-compliance
Lightning Source LLC
Chambersburg PA
CBHW030638220526
45463CB00004B/1571